MY UNDOING

Other books by Aiden Shaw

Brutal (novel)
Boundaries (novel)
Wasted (novel)
*If language at the same time shapes and
    distorts our ideas and emotions, how
    do we communicate love?* (poems)

MY UNDOING

Love in the Thick of Sex, Drugs,
Pornography, and Prostitution

Aiden Shaw

CARROLL & GRAF PUBLISHERS
NEW YORK

My Undoing

Carroll & Graf Publishers
An imprint of Avalon Publishing Group, Inc.
245 West 17th Street, 11th Floor
New York, NY 10011

AVALON
publishing group incorporated

Library of Congress Cataloging-in-Publication Data is available.

ISBN-10: 0-78671-743-2
ISBN-13: 978-0-78671-743-9

9 8 7 6 5

Printed in the United States of America
Interior design by Bettina Wilhelm
Distributed by Publishers Group West

This book is dedicated to everybody in it.

Acknowledgments

I'd like to thank Yuk, Wolfgang, and Joseph Holtzman for helping to actualize this project. Also dear Vicky Heller and Craig Tudhope for getting me through a horrible time that coincided with the editing of this book. Thanks to David, Marc, and Nina for their accounts of events I have no memory of. And to Don Weise, my editor at Carroll & Graf. Most of all I want to thank Patrick Merla for his propagation, nurturing, managing, editing, and educating. Also for his company and sense of humor.

Preface

It's been a continual aspiration of mine not to be ruled by my nature. I felt it wasn't fair who and what I was, and I determined instead to become who and what I wanted to be. I will not let myself regret something because I feel incapable of doing it. I've stood onstage and sung in front of thousands of people, without a good voice and with excruciating sincerity, and I was the shy one in my family. Brought up with strong Catholic beliefs, I've worked as a prostitute and appeared in porn videos as though I thought I was sexy or had any confidence about the way I looked. To really take the piss, I've written about it all in novels and now this memoir, despite wondering if any of it was worth repeating or even remotely useful or in any way entertaining.

The process of writing this book was tough. There are so many ways to look at something. It seemed there was always another layer to peel back, often with more gruesome truths beneath. You may find yourself

disagreeing with my take on something, and you could be right. Sometimes the things I discovered about myself shocked even me. You may
wonder why I'm not more self-aware, intuitive, or shrewd, repeatedly
making mistake after mistake. (And let's be realistic. I'll probably make
the same mistakes again, if not worse.) In fact, I can't believe I've let
anyone see how immature, cruel, thoughtless, evil, and entirely ridiculous I've been. But I am a product of my upbringing, condemned to be
as honest as I'm able, however embarrassing and self-flagellating it
might seem.

This book was written as it happened (at one point typing with only my
right hand while in a wheelchair). I wanted to try a different approach from
that in my novels, to produce something frank, without rumination or
nostalgia. Even so, what I chose to write about wasn't random. I've cut out
not the sex and drugs and what some might consider the extraordinary
parts, but rather the domestic stuff that actually takes up most of my life,
opting instead for things I thought affected me more, always bearing in
mind that people reading this are likely doing so because I've been in porn
movies. Aspiring to dissect my experiences objectively and be philosoph-
ical, all I was finally able to do was testify. None of my demons were exor-
cised, and things I'd rather have forgotten were brought back to life. Once
I'd begun, shit kept happening and I wrote it down, not knowing where
it—or I—was heading. I realized that the truth wasn't just stranger than
fiction but more arbitrary and twisted. Reading over the manuscript, much
of the contents upset me. I cried, literally, for the silly bugger in it.

For the record, I am not a reformed character and I'm not ashamed
of my life so far. I know I'm odd—and that ultimately the joke's on me.

Aiden Shaw
London
February 2006

Part One
Falling

1

I sat in the chair. Within minutes, Chris was pulling his cheeks apart, set-tling onto my dick. With ease, he slid down. Inside him, it was warm. His ass was comfortable, wonderful. I licked his back, wanting to ingest him. His skin gave to my touch, perfect and sensual; his body seemed to mold itself around my fingers. I wanted to permeate him and be absorbed by him. His hairless chest became covered in sweat. Soon we were both drip-ping, slippery, frantic. Our energy rose. My dick was so solid Chris was able to lift off it completely, then sit right back down. He became mon-ster and lamb—ferocious, heated, intense—but still this boy who wanted only to please. We continued to slide and fuck, kissing deeply. Wet hair clung to his neck; sweat trickled down the small of his back to the crease of his ass. All I could see were pretty shapes and colors, my dick going in and out of his white cheeks.

"Stop," I said.

"What's wrong?" said Chris.

"The condom's slipping off."

"Break!" shouted the director. "Condoms!"

A runner was with us in seconds.

"Can I get a Coke as well?" I said to the runner. Then, to Chris: "Do you need anything?"

"No, I'm real fine," he answered with a cheeky smile.

I hadn't particularly planned to do another porn video, but when Al called, I said yes. It didn't take much to persuade me. Maybe there was something seductive about my past that I hadn't been aware of. It helped that it was Al who asked, as I'd always had a soft spot for him, but the most appealing thing was that he was cool about my having HIV. This left me wondering how much the industry had changed in the three years since I'd last done a video. The fact that I said yes was probably an indication that I hadn't.

Now here I was, days into filming, in the middle of my second sex scene and thinking about the model from my first, tormented by the thought of his having sex with other men.

2

I arrived in San Francisco with my friend David, and took a cab directly to our motel just across the road from Al's office. It had the same generic feel as every other motel room I'd ever been in. Nearly every surface had a pattern on it, with landscapes on the wall painted in wisps of beige, blue, and gray. The toilet seat and cups had plastic wraps. The curtains didn't quite meet and were made of a fabric so stiff I presumed they had been fireproofed. The focal point was the television.

Before unpacking, David and I both showered to wash off the airplane smell. In an attempt to rehydrate ourselves, we drank lots of water. We were determined to reduce jet lag by not going to sleep until our usual bedtime. If we managed this, we wouldn't wake up too early the next day. As we settled in for hours of channel surfing and being astounded by American culture, the telephone rang.

"Aiden, I saw you arrive. Welcome." It was Al. "Can you come over for a minute? There's someone I'd like you to meet."

I put on my trainers, glanced quickly in the mirror, and ran across the road, my breathing labored, my body heavy and out of sync. In the office with Al, a man sat with his back to me. He turned.

"This is Hal Stoker," said Al.

My lips went dry; my tongue felt oversized.

The man was perfect: his eyes huge and apologetic, one side of his mouth tipping up, the other too lazy to follow, less confident than a smile but with more meaning.

He stood up, looking anxious. "Please, call me Luke," he said.

"Hey, Luke," I said, feeling awkward.

We shook hands. I hadn't greeted somebody so formally in years, unless as a joke.

"Sit down," said Al.

He started telling us about the video. I heard his words, but my attention was on the man in the chair beside me.

". . . Do you get the idea?"

"Yeah, sure," I said.

"Great. Now to the job at hand." Al turned his chair to face Luke, but continued speaking to me. "Aiden, would you like to work with this man?"

I made a rasping sound.

There was nobody sharper than Al; he'd probably read my response to Luke and was just having fun with the situation. He smiled his warm, sometimes wicked smile, never taking his eyes off Luke.

Luke touched his leg to mine, peered at me out of the corner of his eye. A sensation shot through me, from my knee to my tummy to my crotch to my lips to the muscles around my spine. I turned toward Luke, wanting only to close my eyes, subside, and be engulfed by him.

I tried again, my head loaded with words desperate to voice themselves. All I could manage was a monosyllable.

"Yes."

On the desk were some Polaroids of Luke. I picked them up, planning to feign objectivity and thus appear more professional. Luke looked out from the photos, into me. It was hopeless; I couldn't pretend.

"He's lovely," I said to Al.

"Good," said Al. "If this boy didn't do anything for you, I would have sent you to the doctor for hormones."

I liked Al's warmth, his sense of humor, his ability to find Luke. "Can I keep a Polaroid?" I asked. "To show David, my friend?"

Luke nodded.

"Sure," said Al.

I turned to Luke. "There are no pictures of your bum. Do you have a nice bum?"

"I think so," he said, amused or shy, I couldn't tell which.

"You're so lovely," I said, gazing right at him.

"Thank you," he said, his eyes fixed on mine. I'd thought I couldn't be reached in that way. Often, I found men strange, unknowable. They seemed to speak another language, one of distance, seclusion, and reticence.

Before going to sleep that night, I looked at the Polaroid one more time.
"Isn't he . . ."

"Yeah, yeah, yeah," said David. "*Lovely*."

3

The next day I had to pose for photos for the video box. A driver picked me up at the gym and brought me to the studio, where someone on the floor was fixing a chair. First he, then the rest of the crew, said hello. I sat on a light box and tried to blend in.

"What's your name?" I said to the man on the floor.

"James," he said in a joking, overly macho voice. "We've met before."

"Where?"

"Fire Island, last year. I worked behind the bar. We spoke."

"Oh, yeah," I said. "I didn't recognize you." At the time, he'd had a goatee and a four-inch chrome spike through his nose.

"We met in Miami, too. Last Christmas."

"Right! Sorry. My memory's so bad."

The photographer called me over and said he would be ready for me shortly. I was shown upstairs to a small room where I could undress (so I wouldn't have any underwear marks by the time we started the stills) and relax.

James followed me into the room. "I'm here if you need anything," he said sheepishly.

"Great, thanks."

"I mean, *anything*."

"Oh," I said. "Has Al asked you to help me get a hard-on?"

"You got it."

"Thanks."

"What do you like? Anything special?"

"Kissing works best."

"I'm sure I can manage that. It's a tough job, hey, but somebody's got to do it."

"It's been a long time since I've done this, so . . ."

"Don't worry."

"Sure," I said, with the uncertain intonation of neither an answer nor a question.

From James's expression, it appeared he sensed my doubt. "Listen, I've got stuff to get on with downstairs. Just holler when you need me."

"Cheers," I said, and busied myself with the snacks provided for the models.

James paused at the doorway and said, "Hey!"

"Uh-huh," I said through a mouthful of carrot sticks.

"You'll be fine."

I pulled a big dumb smile, revealing carrot-covered teeth.

"Sexy!" James said, and left. He was meant to be working as a grip, but since there was no filming yet, he mainly got paid for kissing me and sucking my dick to get me hard for the cameras.

On the morning of my first actual scene, I went to the gym early, planning to shower and shave after my workout. I wanted to be in the best shape I could be for the video, so I'd gone to the gym every day in England, even used a personal trainer. A man at the other end of the room was doing dead lifts, his butt and thick legs facing me. He wore red shorts but no T-shirt. When he was finished, he turned around.

It was Luke. I couldn't believe how beautiful he was. In a few hours I would be having sex with him. This seemed odd. And exciting. And scary. I went over to him, feeling ugly and clumsy. The coffee I'd drunk hadn't kicked in; there was still sleep in my eyes. My gym clothes were creased. I looked scruffy. He stood a couple of feet above me, on his machine.

"Hello," I said.

"Hi."

"It's Aiden."

Luke smiled. "I know."

"Last chance to get pretty."

"Yep."

"I wouldn't worry. You look beautiful."

"Thanks."

"Just saying hi. I'll leave you to it. See you later."

Inside I was a mass of questions, some rational, others not—all premature. I got back to my workout.

On the day of shooting a video, instead of concentrating on separate body parts, I usually lightly work my whole body, to kind of wake it up. After showering, shaving, and combing my hair, I thought I looked presentable.

Video companies tend to ask models to arrive long before they're needed, which can be fatal. Handsome men have transformed as I listened to them talk, waiting to do a scene, their personalities making them grotesque. Sex with them became hard work; I'd have to fantasize about somebody else to turn myself on. This wouldn't be a problem with Luke, as I was dying to find out everything about him.

Predictably, my driver was late; when I arrived at the studio, Luke was already preparing to do his stills. These had to be completed before we started filming, while he still looked fresh. (After our scene, he would be sweaty and disheveled, if I had anything to do with it.)

Luke needed help getting a hard-on, and asked if he could suck my dick; within seconds, he was hard. The shoot went smoothly. Every time he needed me, I went on set; I had to do this about fifteen times, but didn't get bored. Luke seemed to employ a series of stock poses and expressions when being photographed. Ordinarily, I would have found this cheesy, but with him I didn't.

When the photographer finished, Luke and I went upstairs. I sat on a chair, Luke on the floor in front of me, affectionately leaning against my legs. He told me about his childhood growing up on a ranch, of riding horses when he was a kid, of a difficult father, and of how he ran away from home at sixteen. We talked for hours. Every now and then one of the camera crew would check to see if we needed anything. At one point, Al popped his head round the door.

"I knew it," he said with a grin, and left.

I had given Al a description of the type of man I wanted to work with, which Luke didn't fit at all. Al had sent me photographs of many different models, but I didn't like any of them. Now here I was, obviously besotted with Luke.

Finally, we were called to the set. It was stark, just a bed with white sheets—very ordinary for a bedroom, but incredibly unusual for a porn set. The floor and walls were painted white, with curved edges to give the illusion of infinity. The lighting was soft, which made Luke's face look airbrushed. We were told to get under the covers and act loving. For me, this wasn't difficult.

It took the crew a long time to get the lighting right. Luke and I talked quietly as we waited, oblivious to our surroundings. By the time we were asked to have sex, I was so into Luke all I wanted to do was kiss him and kiss him and kiss him, only it felt odd being intimate in front of other people. I wanted to be alone with him, not performing.

I decided to simply do my job as well as I could. I'd had years of practice, working as a prostitute, but Luke made it difficult. I couldn't just have sex with him. The look in his eyes pierced me, stirring up feelings I'd never had before.

Filming took hours; by the time we were through, I was physically and emotionally exhausted. And this was only the oral scene. The next day we were to fuck.

A driver dropped us at the motel; we collected David and went to dinner, after which we walked down to the corner of Eighteenth and Castro Streets and I said good night to Luke. David stood a few feet away, giving us privacy.

"You going back to the motel?" Luke asked.

"Yeah," I said, staring at my feet. "But I don't really want to let you go."

Luke lifted my head until our eyes met. "You don't have to."

"What do you mean?"

"You could come to my place."

"I don't want to leave David by himself."

"I could come to your place."

"I'd have to check with David, but would you?"

"Try stopping me."

David agreed to the plan when I assured him that Luke and I wouldn't have sex. I was actually so exhausted that I fell asleep soon after getting into bed.

The next morning, the three of us had breakfast, then went to the gym together. At the studio, I asked Al if Luke and I could go straight into the fucking, before I got too tired from filming face shots and cutaways. Al wanted the best scene he could get, so he agreed.

I bent Luke over and fucked him from behind, remembering to "cheat" my torso toward the camera. (Twisting like this is uncomfortable, but is the way directors prefer.) I flipped Luke onto his back as seamlessly as I could, in case the editors wanted to keep the transition from one position to another.

"Good!" shouted Al. "Now, I want ten minutes of hard fucking."

We did as directed. There was the odd moment when, despite the distractions and pretense, I felt connected, but it was nothing like real sex for me. I wondered what it was like for Luke. When it was time for my cum shot, I aimed the head of my dick toward Luke's bum and squirted onto his left cheek; some cum dribbled down over his hole. I thought it looked perfect, within the context.

We had a break. Luke took a shower, then returned for his cum shot. He knelt in front of me, then over me, and came on my stomach, after which we cleaned up and did our face shots (close-ups of our heads and shoulders as we acted like we were cumming). It was often much more dramatic and noisy than the real thing, so ridiculous I couldn't help smiling. Directors usually didn't mind this. I imagine they thought it looked sweet, even authentic—at least happy.

A driver took us to Luke's apartment, where he showed me his garden, describing in detail his plans for it. That night in bed, after two days of role-playing before the cameras, Luke fucked me. Afterward, we laughed about this.

The next morning, we met David for breakfast at Café Flore on Market Street. He told me that he was returning to England. I wondered why. When Luke was in the toilet, David explained that he felt uncomfortable around Luke and me.

David had been my boyfriend about ten years ago. When we started seeing each other, he stayed over a few nights, then stayed for about eight years. We never actually fell in love; in less than a year, sex faded out and a different kind of relationship evolved. We grew to love each other. (We often traveled together, and once when we were in California we worked in the same video, but not in the same scene. He went on to make others, using the porn name Dave Logan.) I found David beautiful in every respect. He had a tight, muscular body with a bum beyond compare. His hair was blond, his eyes blue. He had perfect white teeth and pretty lips that formed a sweet and genuine smile. And all this was only an intimation of how beautiful he was inside. David was one of the few people I knew who really enjoyed life. He loved the subtle colors in stones, the ugliest insects, the endlessness of space, the complexities of philosophy, and simple things like going for a walk. He inspired me. When all I saw was decay, pain, cynicism, hate—everything wrong and at odds with myself, edges too sharp or too soft—he showed me joy.

David's parents were multimillionaires who gave him an allowance and sent him to the same school as Prince Charles. From there he went to Cambridge University. Sometimes, especially early on in our relationship, it was difficult not to resent him. But my appreciation of him always tipped the balance in his favor. Also, my own life was charmed, as I too received an allowance for years, from a former customer.

My feelings for David ran deep, but my feelings for Luke were urgent. As was David's way, I wasn't faced with the dilemma of choosing whom I should spend time with, because he'd already decided what he would do.

The rest of the day was spent on B-roll footage consisting of me running shirtless through deserted streets, after which I went back to Luke's. The following morning he tried to fuck me again, but it hurt too much, so instead he sat on my dick and came on my stomach. I asked if I could taste his cum. He bent over, kissed my stomach, then kissed my lips.

We met David for breakfast again, this time at the Cove Café on Market Street. At one point I went to the toilet. When I came back, he and

Luke were silent. Later, Luke told me they hadn't said a word while I was gone. David left that afternoon. I couldn't see him off because I was shooting more B-roll. This time, I was naked in Golden Gate Park, digging a grave and burying myself.

4

I drifted out of sleep to a strange sensation. I was being held upright in bed; something warm pushed gently against my lips. It smelled good. I gave in and it entered my mouth: a sweet taste. I let it continue, my senses telling me it was okay. I tasted butter and sugar, noted the texture. An idea of cake formed. I opened my eyes.

Luke held me, parentlike, feeding me. He'd gotten up very early—he had to be at work at a coffee shop at six—and heated cake in the microwave for me and melted butter on it. I couldn't think of a nicer way to be woken. I felt lovely. Loved.

Luke had to leave soon, but first we had sex. He came; I didn't. I was doing another scene that day. Luke lay beneath me, a faint smile on his face, my dick inside him. I wanted to stay that way forever.

Finding the model for my second scene had been difficult. I didn't like any of the photos I was shown. In the end, I agreed to choose a model on the set, one of the three others in the scene.

Intentionally, I arrived at the studio late, knowing it took at least four hours to set up. The other models were already getting to know one another. As I walked into the room, I was taken aback. One of the models reminded me of Luke. His screen name was Chris Rock. He was handsome in a boy-you-might-have-gone-to-school-with kind of way, and seemed very excited.

Another model worked under the name of Todd Gibbs; his white, unblemished body was the most perfectly proportioned I'd ever seen. In contrast, his movements were brittle, his manner blank, his communication curt.

The last model was James, who'd helped me with my hard-on for the photo shoot. He was a nice guy, but it would take more than being nice to counteract the long hours and uncomfortable positions we would probably deal with that day.

I sat quietly, hoping the others would do the same. Chris appeared raring to go, Todd acted cool, and James was clearly nervous. We spoke, but very casually, basic stuff like where we each were from. This seemed to go on for hours. At one point James mentioned that our scene was a four-way. I was surprised, but didn't let on.

I went downstairs and spoke to Al. He told me his assistant had sorted out the whole thing. This was strange. I found the assistant and asked him what was going on. He acted confused and said that Al knew. Something was wrong, or somebody was lying. I got Al and brought him to the assistant, and confronted them. It turned out a four-way had been planned. I told them I wouldn't do it. Diplomatically, Al asked what I would do.

"I'll work with Todd," I said.

"I think you'd rather work with Chris," Al said.

"No," I said firmly.

"Aiden, believe me, you want to work with Chris."

Finally realizing what he meant, I said, "Al, I'll tell you one more time. I'll work with Chris or not at all."

He laughed, I think pleased with the outcome.

Despite the mix-up, and beyond most things in my life, I trusted Al's taste. Knowing him as I did, I wouldn't have put it past him to have thought up this whole muddle in order to make me choose at least one of the models.

Hours later, we all went down to the set—the same white infinity, but this time with a black chair instead of the bed, and a green leather-and-chrome bench behind it. Once in position and prepped by Al, Chris and I began to kiss. Despite my feelings for Luke, my dick quickly got hard.

Al noticed this. The crew were still fussing with the lighting, but a hard dick on set is God. The artist in Al subsided and the porn director kicked in. "We have a hard-on," he announced.

The crew responded to one of the ten commandments of shooting porn with due reverence, leaving what they were doing or just making it do. Within minutes they were in their filming personas.

"Okay, everybody," Al said; then, specifically to the models: "We're going to start shooting, guys. Remember where the camera is."

Pause.

"Rolling."

Another pause.

"And . . . action!"

I stood in front of the chair. Chris sucked my dick. Jesus, he was pretty. After about fifteen minutes of this, I sat on the chair and Chris climbed astride me, facing me, his lovely bum hovering over my dick. I so wanted to just ease him down. It didn't take long to switch from internal and consumed by Luke to external and amazed by Chris. It helped that he seemed into me; I liked nothing less than a model who was indifferent.

Either Chris was really enjoying himself or he was a good actor. Whichever the case, it was the most intense sex I'd ever had on a set.

When we broke for a new condom, I shouted to Al, "Is it okay?" He nodded, smiling mischievously.

James and Todd had to break as well, for we were all in the same shot. They'd been behind us, fucking on the bench, but I was so engrossed in Chris, I hadn't noticed. After a swig of Coke, which Al referred to as "pecker power," the camera rolled again.

Chris and I did pretty much as we pleased. From the sitting position facing me, he turned and faced away. The view of his smooth little bum easily compensated for my not being able to see his face. I lowered him onto my dick. Fuck! He stood up. I pursued him, I think; it was hard to tell who was leading whom. I leaned him forward and fucked him awhile in that position. He lowered himself onto his hands, then his knees, and we did the classic doggy position, fucking until I could barely hold it any longer.

"Can I cum, Al?" I shouted.

He responded first to the cameraman—"A tight shot, please"—then to me. "Knock yourself out, Aiden. And give me some noise."

I focused all my attention on my dick pumping in and out of Chris's bum. I bent forward, licked sweat off his back, fucked him some more, then pulled my dick from his ass and flicked off the condom, groaning as though for Chris's benefit but really as a signal for the crew to close in on the small of Chris's back, his tiny waist, his smooth skin and hairless bum. Then I came.

As soon as Chris and I were done, the camera moved to Todd and James. I stood behind Al, to see how the scene looked in the monitor. He turned his head and made an expression of disinterest. I was glad it wasn't me on the screen. It would be some time before they finished, so I headed upstairs to get dressed, relax, and phone Luke. Chris stayed behind to watch the rest of the scene.

Although Chris was completely sexy, I was glad it was over. I felt a sense of achievement. When Todd and James had finished shooting, they and Chris ate and got dressed while the crew packed up.

We were all taken to wherever we wanted to go. I went back to Luke's and was surprised to find him waiting, looking pleased to see me. I still had B-roll footage to shoot, but the scene with Chris had been my last sex scene in the movie. Luke and I celebrated with a nice dinner out.

When I left San Francisco—more important, when I left Luke—I felt sad, excited, yet hopeful. This soon melted aboard the airplane into a Valium-induced, not-bothered-by-anything feeling. Once home and recovered from jet lag, all I could think about was Luke. It wasn't long before I was on a plane heading back to San Francisco.

5

Bad timing. Luke's new escort ad had just appeared in the *Bay Area Reporter*, and his pager went off constantly. Every time he answered, I felt anxious. Instead of bottling it up, I told Luke.

"I hate thinking of you with a customer."

"So don't think about it."

"I can't help it. You speak to them so often."

"Everyone gets at me about my work."

"Baby, I don't have a problem with prostitution."

"Then what is the problem?"

"I'm not sure. I guess I feel protective, but jealous also. I know that I enjoyed it, sometimes."

"Well, I don't."

"What about the movies?"

"What about them?"

"Sometimes the models are lovely. Look who I got."

"I'm not about to fall for anyone else."

"Why?"

"You're my baby, Rufus. Don't you get it?"

I didn't know where the name Rufus came from, but I liked it. Luke tousled my hair.

"Rufus, *you're* my baby. You've no reason to feel insecure. But please, don't ask me to change my life. I wouldn't do that for anybody."

This shocked me. At the same time, I admired him. I had both good and bad memories of prostitution, but was certain it had made me remote—the last thing I wanted Luke to be with me.

"I'm sorry, baby," I said, feeling awkward. "I won't mention it again."

Luke could see I was upset, and gave me a hug. We were on a particularly busy shopping street, but I was lost in his arms.

This addressed, but in no way dealt with things. The rest of the trip was nice, if often interrupted. Luke agreed to visit me in London. We chose a date when I would be doing a gig with my band, Whatever.

Just before going to San Francisco to work on the movie, I'd been asked by Sean Strub to guest edit *Poz*, a magazine about HIV and AIDS he published in New York. I'd never edited a magazine before, and felt I had something to add to the debate. "My issue," as I called it (even though Elizabeth Taylor was on the cover, making my input and opening essay seem meager in comparison), was to be the first time *Poz* would be available in England, so I was asked to perform with my band at the launch party.

I went home to prepare for the gig and wait the two weeks for Luke's arrival.

6

Luke's plane landed very early in the morning. After letting him sleep a couple of hours, I woke him, because later that evening Whatever were playing at Substation Soho, a club run by my friend Wayne Shires, and Luke wanted to come to the sound check.

At Substation, I introduced Luke to Nina and Marc, Whatever's other lead vocalists, as well as two of my closest friends. Nina was primarily a writer and bass player whose résumé also included a world championship medal in martial arts. Until recently she'd been a sex worker but had eased out of it when she discovered she could earn enough to get by on doing the things she truly enjoyed—singing, playing bass, and tumbling (she worked most summers in a circus, usually on the high wire, but once playing a clown, which included riding a tiny bike). Marc, while easier to describe—a visual artist, a vegetarian, and in therapy—was more complex, with masses of stuff in his head that only occasionally escaped as art. The three of us had different styles of singing and performing. Nina also played bass guitar. Our lead guitarist, Matt Fisher, could play in any style. We liked his versatility and the fact that he was user-friendly. Our keyboard player, Neil, had attended the Royal College of Music and was considered by many to be a genius. He could simulate everything from strings to drum loops. Sometimes we used a live drummer as well, a sweet man called Jay. Finally, any of our friends who wanted to join us onstage could do so. This often included a man called S, who would mime the songs.

After the sound check, we ate and killed time, then got ready at a friend's place on Old Compton Street in Soho. Nina had her hair done Afro-style and wore what she called her seventies prison warden drag: brown pencil skirt, a man's white shirt with the collar open, and brown lace-up high heels. Marc had spiky, pale green hair and wore a National Health back support he'd lived in since falling off his horse a few years before. My head was shaved, and with makeup I created a big cold sore and heavy black bags under my eyes. Marc wrote DOG FUCKER in black marker all over my arms.

We made our way back to Substation. Nina had already paid the soundman, who showed up stoned on heroin, and may as well have not bothered returning. We couldn't hear ourselves onstage, and the audience seemed to hear even less. Having been assured the lighting would be sorted out, we hadn't bothered worrying about it. We should have known better—there wasn't any. My younger brother Des, who'd come with his wife, Lucy, realized we were having trouble and attempted to rescue us by picking up a light from the front of the stage and beaming it on us. Where it had been shining previously, I couldn't tell you.

We tried our best, but it was a shitty gig. At the end of the set, I stepped forward off the stage into the front row—and Luke's arms. He caught me and kissed me.

We hung around the club doing drugs. At some point while Luke was dancing, Nina, Marc, and I found ourselves in a broom closet with Princess Julia (the DJ that night) and a woman she was seeing, who looked like a poster boy for Hitler Youth and had a sexy, East End–bloke appeal. Julia had several defining qualities. One was her kooky sense of humor; you almost had to guess when she was joking. Another was her voice, which had a common, market-trader lilt to it, except the things she said were always so clever, with a viewpoint you hadn't thought of yet. Then there was the way she dressed. When Julia constructed a look, she nailed it with precision and detail. She was always at least six months (sometimes a year or more) ahead of what you saw on catwalks or in fashion magazines. This night she was wearing a gold T-shirt that clung to her body like paint, emphasizing her perfect breasts, nipples, and youthful figure.

I'm guessing that we were in the cupboard for privacy, because we were doing drugs, although Julia was one of the few people I liked (not counting parents and friends in recovery) who didn't do any. She must have been just hanging out with us. She was one of the very few people I could be messy high with—she was able to go with the flow (if anything, she seemed to find it amusing). The rest of us did K and coke. I mentioned how beautiful Julia looked and for some reason suggested that we all swap T-shirts. Julia got the one I'd worn onstage, perhaps not a good deal, but she wore it so well it hardly mattered. Nina got Julia's, and was very happy with the trade. I got Nina's, which was from the seventies and said I WILL BE RICH AND FAMOUS, with the WILL BE crossed out and changed to AM. Julia's girlfriend and Marc must have got each other's shirts. By the time we left the cupboard we were all dressed differently, and relatively happy, if not a bit bewildered, with the outcome.

We were having such a good time at the club, with so many people we liked having turned up to support us. Because we'd disappointed them horribly onstage we wanted to party on. Flora, another of my close friends and our drummer Jay's girlfriend, invited us to her place. Messy as we all were, everybody managed to make it there. The inventory wasn't A-list, nor even B-, C-, D-, or E-list (although a lot of those pills were circulating), but it *was* double F (for Fabulous Freaks) -list. It seemed all of London's finest (as I liked to call them) were there, including:

– Steven Maguire, a self-confessed paddy of the old and new school. Old in that he had a close, protective extended family who, if standing arm-to-arm, would have reached back to Ireland. New because he was stylish beyond comprehension. Unlike S, who tended to look deranged, Steven could put together the oddest assortment of clothes and make you feel cool just being seen with him. He had a "divil" of a personality (as he referred to it). He could walk into a packed, boisterous, drunken straight crowd and within minutes have them laughing at his antics. Nothing intimidated Steven.

– Richard Tory (whose house we'd got ready at earlier and with whom I'd done the odd bit of recording). He was a clothes designer from way back, and had been recording music for years. Along with the truly original Leigh Bowery—to my mind the most incredible club/freak/modern-artist/fashion-iconoclast ever—Richard had formed the original line-up of a band called Minty. He was also one of many who had played with Whatever, and also been a DJ. He'd lived in the heart of Soho since before it became London's version of the Castro or the West Village. I never saw him without a kooky hairstyle. The one he favored at the time of the party was a six- or seven-inch red spike that stuck straight out from the crown of his head. Conversely, he was meek, pleasant, nervous—a classic quiet, unassuming eccentric.

– Miss Kimberly, glamorous club hostess/actress/personality I'd met many years ago at a club called Taboo, when she was still a beautiful boy fresh from New York with dreams of making it as a runway model.

– Stuart Who, journalist not only finding his feet as an international DJ playing circuit parties all over the world, but (more significantly to me) able to get my weary body moving when he played a set, which was quite an achievement.

– Mathew Glamore was many things, one of them being the founder of a group of musicians, writers, singers, and performance artists known as the Offset. He was a club freak with a difference: he had a vision. Neither he nor anybody else knew what it was, but I believe that whether performing a concert, organizing something, or simply running what he thought was a great new club night, he felt inspired to do so. It was the art that counted, never the money.

– Suzi Gruger had gained notoriety in London by starting some of the first hardcore post-AIDS-hysteria sex clubs. One of her more famous was Fist, where backrooms weren't necessary and anything-goes sexual behavior was expected. The dress code was *fuck*, and most obliged.

– Neil Kazor, our keyboard player, was there with his boyfriend Kenny C, another popular London DJ. They were as odd a couple as you could meet, telling me once how both their grandparents—one German, the other Jewish—had been in Auschwitz.

Who else was at the party?

– Marc's beautiful nephew Ryan, with an equally beautiful school-mate (we could have made a fortune for the pair on the black market).

– Andy Sticks, a man who sometimes performed with us but did his own fast-talking skeptical poetry. He had model good looks, with the grandeur of a different age, but he preferred not to work this aspect of himself. His mind was sharp and his tongue, too, but instead of bitching he used these in his poetry.

– Mark Langy ran ff, the most popular late-night club for gays in the mid-nineties (the initials stood for "First Friday," not the same meaning many attach to them), and a bar/theater/gallery called Freedom. In addition to being singer Marc Almond's manager, he was a part-time fireman studying fire forensics. Unlike most of the people at the party, he could get all the attention he wanted by merely sitting still, and he knew it.

This leads me to the party's host, Flora. I first saw her at Freedom, standing in front of one of her huge photocopied art pieces looking puzzled and curious, as though she were seeing it for the first time, but also looking like a movie star rather than an artist, a seductive combo. Flora was a tiny girl with the whitest skin, blonde hair like a baby's, and the kind of lips some people pay a fortune to obtain. She was graceful and serious, with an affectionate warmth that made you want to kiss, cuddle, and love her. I introduced myself and stuck to her ever after. A few times, I got her to sing one of my songs onstage with Whatever, but she was so uneasy that she sang with a timid voice. It was heartbreakingly genuine and beautiful.

A couple of dealers were at the party. Acid seemed one of the favorites that night, so everybody was more disordered than usual. People had collective baths, spilling drinks over each other by accident, then because they thought it looked good. Messy seemed to be the order of the evening. Everybody shouted stories, each thinking theirs was funnier, but nobody cared about making sense. Some people left and came back with reinforcements—other dealers, booty from shops that served alcohol illegally after hours—each person at least as ludicrous as the next.

Russell, Nina's boyfriend, took just enough acid to want to sit under the piano most of the evening. Taking advantage of the presence of this large musical instrument, Nina stood on top of it and sang Edith Piaf—a cappella, of course, with the original French lyrics—while simultaneously doing contortionist acrobatics. She and Russell made a nice couple, affectionate but not so it made anybody uncomfortable.

The party dragged on until, group by group, we all escaped. When Luke and I finally got home, I heated milk for hot chocolate and we sat together on the sofa and drank it, dazed. I had a bath to remove Marc's DOG FUCKERs from my arms, brushed my teeth, and got ready for bed as quickly as possible. Before rejoining Luke, I went into the living room and searched in a drawer.

When Luke heard me coming he lifted the covers for me to get in bed beside him. I climbed in on top of him, my legs between his. He was naked, felt warm, and smelled sweet. We squeezed each other and kissed briefly. I nuzzled into his neck and chest, then made my way down his torso until I lay with my face at the base of his tummy, just above his crotch. Suddenly my eyes filled with tears and my body trembled.

"Baby, what's wrong?" he said, surprised.

I started to cry.

"Baby," he repeated, this time concerned.

"I . . . want to give you this," I managed to say, uncurling my fingers and placing my gift in his hand. "It's my mum's engagement ring. She gave it to me on my nineteenth birthday."

Luke was silent for a moment, then said, "Rufus, you can't give me this."

"Do you understand why I'm giving it to you?"

"Because you like me?"

"No, baby, because I love you."

Silent again, Luke squeezed me tight, pulling back the covers until we were both exposed. I lifted his hand to his face, to show him the ring.

"I saw this ring every day as I grew up. I want it to be a reminder to you, whatever you're doing—serving coffee, working out, even crying—that you are loved."

I'd never expected to feel this way in my life. Why should I? It had never happened before.

"I love you, too," Luke said.

Which made me cry harder.

7

For several years I rented an apartment in Miami's South Beach in December and January to avoid the long, bleak English winters. David decided to join me this year. Being with him should have been blissful, but it wasn't. Luke visited.

The more attached I became to Luke, the less happy I was. This was no fault of Luke's; his only error was that he'd met me. Obviously, I was pleased at the thought of being with him, but I became infatuation personified: clingy, paranoid, needy. Nothing Luke gave was enough for me. I always wanted more. More time, more attention, more affirmation. It wasn't attractive.

Nina arrived in mid-December. Luke had a tummy bug, so I went to the airport alone to pick her up. She looked stunning emerging from customs in a long dress that was a bit too eveningwear for a flight but effortless all the same. (I think it had something to do with her attitude.

Whatever she wore, she always looked cool and hot at the same time.) Her hair was naturally black, breast-length, and shampoo-ad thick. As a rule, she was dynamic, exciting, and tough, somebody you wouldn't have liked to be on the wrong side of at school. Not that she was aggressive— unless she was protecting herself or a friend; then there'd be bloodshed before she'd give in.

The next morning, David, Luke, and I had breakfast with Nina at the Eleventh Street Diner, then showed her around Miami until the sun had risen properly, whereupon we headed toward the Twelfth Street Beach, which was only blocks from my apartment. The Twelfth Street Beach was the gay beach; if a circuit party was on, it felt like a gay club.

David lasted as long as it took to have a swim, dry naturally, then have another swim. Although he liked the T-shirt-and-shorts weather of Miami, he wasn't keen on getting too much sun. He preferred to sit indoors with a book and the air-conditioning on high. It wasn't long before Nina left us, too, saying that she'd meet us later at the apartment. I assumed she was just restless, excited to be somewhere new. It didn't occur to me that she might not like being around me and Luke. Nina and I usually had such fun together, but now Luke permeated my every thought, got all my attention. I found it difficult to focus on Nina. But she was resourceful, and I assumed she wouldn't let something as tedious as my infatuation get in the way of her having fun.

Left alone with hundreds of near-naked men, Luke and I sweated, turned over on our blanket, drank water, and talked. As hard as I tried to appreciate what the beach had to offer, all I was capable of doing was obsessing about the photo shoot Luke had scheduled for February.

"I can get used to you doing punters," I told him.

"That wouldn't be a problem here anyway."

"Why?"

"I didn't place my ad in time."

"Shit!" I said, feeling relieved.

"I'll have no money."

"We'll be okay."

"I don't want to scrounge off you."

"Let's just see what happens?"

"It's all right for you to be so casual. I've got January's rent to pay."

"Don't worry, baby. I'll cover it."

"At least I've got that photo session in February."

"I won't be there."

"So?"

"You'll need somebody to help you get hard."

"And?"

"That makes me feel weird."

"I don't understand how you fit into this."

"You're turned on by them. That's the whole idea, right?"

"Yeah, but that doesn't mean much. It's work."

"It's not just an excuse to have sex with other people?"

"Baby, you knew when I met you what I did for a living."

"What I'm trying to say is, *I* don't need anyone else."

"I don't *need* anyone else, either."

"Sorry. I don't *want* anyone else."

"Let's go for a swim."

The conversation was over.

Normally, Luke swam far out from shore. This time, he held on to me in the water. He pulled down my swimming shorts, and I did the same to his. We kissed, our bodies slipping against each other. I became unaware of the beach, the clenched abs, the bitching, the manufactured nonchalance. I felt so loved.

Luke had a way of affecting me like no one ever had. I'd become soft in his arms, moved by everything he said or did. This probably sounds good, but it meant that when away from him I felt pointless, which gave me little option but to be around him. It didn't occur to me to question how Luke felt. I got the impression that he valued me, possibly even wanted me to be the one he came home to—but after what and who?

Luke seemed capable of real openness, which was modern, gay, logical. Part of me wanted to be more like him. Another part couldn't bear the thought of him having sex with anybody else. It was probably easy for others to see the imbalance in our interest for each other, but with bossy, brutal, heavy-handed chemicals like serotonin and dopamine at the helm of my reason, I found it impossible to have a single clear thought.

On New Year's Eve, we went to the Delano Hotel, where New York club host Suzanne Bartsch was throwing a party. At the beginning of the evening I hung out in her chalet chatting with Rupert Everett, whom I knew from London. As the night progressed, I met various club kids who'd been shipped down from New York as decoration for the party, each as clichéd as the next. But one of them was also a musician and performer, and we spoke about our bands and making music. At midnight, Luke wanted to be among the crowd—completely understandable—and I wanted to hold the man I was in love with—equally understandable, but unfortunately different.

A dealer I'd met the year before invited us to a club called Salvation. Since the Delano party was nearly over, we agreed to go. First, however, he wanted to stop at his apartment to pick up supplies. There we met his roommate Ashley, the kind of man you wouldn't notice in a crowd but who, in a small apartment with no distractions, high on G and crystal, seemed immensely desirable.

At Salvation, Luke took off his shirt, unbuttoned the top of his trousers, climbed onto a podium, and danced sexily, like a stripper. I was embarrassed, but I knew he enjoyed it. I left him to it, busying myself talking with David and Nina until a bunch of men and women came back with us to my apartment, where we finished off what drugs we had—G, Special K, cocaine, crystal—then called all the local dealers we knew for refills. No one answered. I thought this unprofessional the morning following New Year's Eve.

Luke disappeared with Ching, a woman we'd befriended at Salvation, who took him up to the roof and showed him her cunt. Meanwhile, I got to know Ashley. Luke had told me he wanted to have sex with us. I pictured Luke kissing Ashley, which gave me a strange sensation in my stomach. Intimacy and sex had been toyed with too much in my life; I wanted a monogamous boyfriend. The problem was, I was much more open-minded when high, and I felt comfortable with Ashley—though this, too, was probably because I was high. The more I looked at him, the more I enjoyed doing so; the closer I got, the more I noticed that was worth getting close to.

Finished with Luke on the roof, Ching took Nina for a drive. New Year's Eve dragged on till the afternoon and evening, and only then did everybody finally leave.

Luke, Ashley, and I were alone, and it wasn't long before we were naked and fucking. Neither Luke nor Ashley could get a hard-on. I could, so I felt at least useful. Regardless of being busy constantly, feeling some incredible sensations, and seeing some perfectly beautiful images, I couldn't quite manage to lose myself in the action. When breaking to pee or for a drink, I'd imagine how my relationship with Luke would be affected. Ashley was great sex, but I can't say I had fun. By the time he left, over six hours later, I felt cold toward him. More significantly, I felt cold toward Luke. But I got ready for bed as though it were an ordinary evening, and within a short time found the peace of mind I sought in a tablet-induced sleep.

When we woke, we ate supper with David at the Eleventh Street Diner. I had oatmeal and red wine, hoping it would act as a sedative. We used the little energy the meal afforded us to get home and back into bed. New Year's-Goddamn-Eve was finally over.

8

For several days we saw Nina only when she popped into our apartment to change clothes. On each visit she seemed increasingly obsessive and compulsive. From my experience of crystal, I guessed Nina hadn't slept from one visit to the next.

Finally I decided it was time to return to the gym, regardless of how I felt. David still wasn't up to it, but I persuaded Luke to join me. Afterward, we had lunch on Lincoln Mall, a pedestrian road popular with tourists.

I spotted Tristan, a man I'd met several years ago at Kinky Gerlinky, a party in London. I'd never liked him much, but when he stopped to talk it wasn't difficult to be nice to him. He now lived in South Beach and ran an escort agency. I expressed interest, hoping to get work for Luke. Tristan took our details and we swapped numbers.

That night, Tristan called with a job for me in Fort Lauderdale. I accepted it, thinking that if I worked, Luke wouldn't have to, but also—I hate to admit it—because I wanted Luke to feel how I felt when he did this to me.

A driver named Liam picked me up at ten o'clock. I felt something between us instantly. Liam had the skin of a child and brand new–looking lips that moved seductively, as if aware they were being watched. I wondered if they'd experienced as many meaningless kisses as mine had.

We made casual chitchat as he drove. After a while, Liam said, "Fasten your seatbelt. Already, I care enough to say this." He looked serious.

"Do you?"

"Yes." Then: "You've made me miss the turnoff."

"I don't care how long this journey takes," I said. "I'm enjoying myself."

"Me, too."

Still he looked serious. As we neared our destination, I began to feel anxious.

"I forgot to bring condoms," I said.

"So don't fuck him."

"I hope he's not expecting it."

"If he wants to get fucked, he should have condoms."

"Would you?"

"Cheeky! And how would that situation occur?"

"What I meant was, do you really think it's his responsibility?"

Liam pulled up outside a hotel between a tangle of freeways. I felt uncomfortable. What if I couldn't get a cab back to South Beach? What if . . .

"Would you like me to wait for you?" said Liam.

"It's not necessary."

"I'd like to."

"What will you do?"

"I'll go to Target."

"I love Target."

"I might take you, one day."

"How romantic."

"I'll be back in an hour."

"Are you sure?"

"As sure as I am of you," said Liam. This took me aback.

"Give me an hour and a quarter, just to be on the safe side."

"Okay. If you're going to be longer, come out and tell me."

I opened the car door, stepped onto the sidewalk, and looked back at Liam. "I appreciate this," I said.

"I hope so. It's meant to make you like me."

"It works."

"Soon you'll find you can't live without me."

It all came back as I walked straight past the reception desk to the elevator: how to be a good whore. Be inconspicuous.

Floor five, room ten. I knocked. Shuffling behind the door.

When it opened, my first thoughts were of the man's roundness—his face, his tummy, even his fingers. He introduced himself as Mike, offering his hand to shake. I took it, struck by his humility, and acting as much like a nice, sexy man as I could. At the same time, I was distracted. Every past cum splat, beer spill, piss-and-shit mishap seemed present in the room, though presumably a maid cleaned after each customer.

Mike offered me a beer and I accepted—anything to blur the situation. I sat in an armchair, a device I always use, knowing the punter can't sit next to me; only when I'm ready do I join him on the sofa or suggest moving into the bedroom. I swigged my beer as he explained his fantasy: I should find him sexy and be firm with him. Once the logistics were out of the way, we began to open up to each other. Looking at the floor, he told me of his wife, a scrub nurse. He seemed so rare, yet completely average, and easy to love. Feeling genuine affection, I went and sat beside him, putting my hand on his knee. He smiled. In return, I told him about my relationship with Luke. We talked for three-quarters of an hour before I thought to remind him that time was running out.

"I'd like you to stay a couple of hours," he said.

"I'm afraid I can't. I have a driver waiting."

"I want you to be comfortable."

"I am."

"It's a shame you can't stay longer."

"We could meet again. Next time, I could plan to spend a couple of hours."

"Okay. Should I call the agency?"

"It's probably best."

I pulled him to me and pressed his head against my chest. He groaned, rubbing his face petlike into my stomach, making his way to my crotch.

"Shall we go into the bedroom?" I said.

"Please."

We took off our clothes. I had on a cock ring, so my dick was full of blood. I felt I looked the part. He sucked me for a while. I put my fingers inside his mouth, pulled his face to my balls and told him to lick them. I stood on the bed and turned around so he could see my back and bum, then crouched slowly onto his face. Frenzied panting, sucking. Snuffling noises. He began to tremble. I sat down heavily. Some convulsing beneath me, then he was still. Five minutes later, I was out of the building. Liam's smile was easy to see, even from a distance.

"How was it? Was he difficult?"

"No. He gave me two hundred dollars extra. I like that in a customer."

"I got some mouthwash for you."

"What for? All he did was suck my dick, balls, and ass." Part of me hoped Liam was picturing this.

He stalled a moment, then said, "You're kidding."

"No."

"Wow. Easy, hey?"

"I don't know."

Liam looked confused by my reply, then another thought seemed to override this. He looked straight ahead, then at me.

"I got you something else. Maybe it's not the right time."

"Show me."

Somewhat reluctantly, he pulled from behind his seat a heart-shaped box of chocolates, and handed it to me.

"What's this for?"

"Valentine's Day?"

"That's still a month off. What are you saying?"

"Nothing."

"This means nothing?"

"No," he said. "I mean it's no big deal. But, it is something."

"Yeah," I said. "It's really nice."

We ate the chocolates as we drove to Miami.

The back of the car was full of stuff. Liam explained that he was in the middle of moving. I told him I would help him, then called Luke from Liam's mobile phone and let him know what I was up to.

We managed to get everything in the lift in one go. Liam's apartment was on the sixteenth floor. A balcony overlooked the beach. Liam followed me onto it with two glasses of orange juice. Neon lights from the hotels on Ocean Drive glowed in the clear night sky: lovely, mesmerizing.

I looked at Liam's fine profile. He turned to me and said, "Would you like to kiss me?"

I couldn't help smiling. "Yes, I would, but . . ."

"You've got a boyfriend?"

"That's right," I said. Then, seeing his response: "Come here."

Our bodies slotted together perfectly in a hug, the soft skin of his neck pressed against my face. As lovely as this felt, it wasn't difficult to pull away.

He started to speak, then stopped. After a few seconds, he said, "Can I see you again?"

"Of course, but you know the deal."

"I do. I like you, Aiden. You're not like the guys I usually meet here. They always just want to get me in bed."

"You poor thing," I said jokingly.

"They're so fast, it scares me sometimes. It was different in Minnesota."

I found this adorable, and reached for him and hugged him again, then slowly released him and stepped back.

"Let me give you a lift home."

"That'll be great."

As we pulled up outside my apartment, Liam took my hand, lacing his fingers through mine. "Can I call you?" he asked.

By now a little confused, I said, "Sure."

Inside, I found a different Luke from the one I'd left. He gave me more of his attention than usual and said, "I love you, Aiden." It was rare for Luke to instigate this sentence; even on the phone with his mum, it was always a reply: "I love you, too."

"What's brought this on?" I said.

"This Liam guy. I get the feeling you like him." I was silent, amazed at Luke's intuition. He looked earnest. "I don't want to lose you."

My thoughts shot from one to another. Was Luke jealous? Had this been my goal? I sighed. Was I scheming, and was this something I'd have to get used to if I wanted to navigate a boyfriend? I didn't like the idea.

9

Two days later, Tristan called with another job for me, this time a few streets away, within walking distance. The appointment was for midnight. Before I left, I took a beer from the fridge. Sipping on it, I tried to relax, letting my mind fantasize about what the customer might be like. From experience, I knew this wasn't realistic, but I indulged myself. Luke sat silently watching me, apparently uneasy. I kissed him good-bye and left.

The punter's apartment was in the same building as Liam's, on the opposite side, so I knew where the lift was. I pressed the button for the twenty-sixth floor, got out, rang the punter's bell. When he opened the door, I was surprised to find him quite good-looking, with a pretty torso, worked-out arms, and a cute if droopy and doglike face. He introduced himself as Jim.

"Would you like a glass of wine?" he asked.

"Sure," I said.

"Red okay?"

"My favorite."

Jim headed out of the room, I guessed toward the kitchen.

"Your money's on the table," he said loudly.

My head turned reflexively. The money was on a chrome-and-glass table.

"Cheers," I said.

I picked up the cash, folded it, and put it in my pocket. Cutlery drawer and cupboard noises followed. I studied the room. Cream carpet spread diseaselike on the floor; where it stopped, an equally cream sofa took over, which, relentless, smeared into the cream wall behind. The apartment felt like a sensory vacuum, as though it hadn't been colored in. My eyes were drawn to the floor-to-ceiling windows and doors, through which I could see blackish sky—not a color technically, but at least it wasn't cream. I heard a *chink*.

Jim handed me a glass of wine, smiling. I smiled back and took the drink.

"What do you do?" I said, stalling, using up time.

"Interior design."

In a sitcom, I would have spat out my drink. This décor was intentional? Maybe Jim didn't like to bring his work home with him. My mind spun. Was it a joke that went over my head? Or was I the joke, or was Jim just messing with me?

I turned to the sliding door onto the balcony to distract myself and disguise my feelings, hoping my action would read as confidence and that Jim would appreciate this. The opening door made a gritty noise, probably sand. Night air entered the room, reassuring and welcoming me. I stepped outside. Jim followed, obviously proud of the view. Below us on the bay I could see man-made private islands and a huge, docked cruise ship. A tiny disco boat chugged by, its multicolored lights flashing. Maybe because I wasn't used to views, or maybe because of its contrast with the monotonous room, I appreciated it even more than Liam's view—and Liam had distracted me, whereas I was happy to be distracted from Jim. "What a view," I said, thinking it was expected of me, not bothering to come up with something original.

"It's why I bought the place," said Jim, I assumed to inform me that he owned rather than rented the apartment.

"Right," I said, nodding knowingly.

Chat done with, it was time to get down to business. "Follow me," Jim said, and led me through the living room into his bedroom and yet more clichéd décor.

"Any chance of another drink?" I said.

"Finished already?"

"Yeah," I said.

"One mo'," he said.

"Great," I said, thinking how I hadn't heard the expression "mo'" since I was at school.

In this room the cream was sprinkled with Ralph Lauren and antique clutter. I spotted poppers and a bullet on a chest of drawers.

"You're quite the drinker," said Jim when he returned.

"Quite the everything," I said.

"We'll have fun, then," he said, looking me up and down.

"I'm sure," I said, thinking the opposite.

Jim passed me my drink and I took a large gulp, visualizing red wine on cream carpet. We both smiled. This made me uncomfortable.

I acted relaxed. "What's in the bullet?"

"K. Do you want some?"

"Sure," I said.

He handed me the bullet and I took two bumps.

"A pro," he said. "No pun intended."

"Don't worry," I said. "None taken."

He laughed unconvincingly.

I pulled off my T-shirt, feeling tanned, sexy, a good value, then sat on the bed to remove my jeans. Jim undressed completely, never taking his eyes off me. My jeans shed, suddenly Jim was beside me, kneeling, moving my hands away from my underwear, pulling them down, his face hovering over my dick.

"May I?" he said, as though in an entirely different situation, but obviously referring to my now plump dick.

"It would be my pleasure," I said, imitating his weird Victorian politeness.

"The pleasure is all mine," he said, his mouth moving toward his target.

I lay back, feeling the K and the inside of Jim's mouth. He sucked my dick and balls, licked the tops of my legs. Part of me became pure physicality, another registered the bedposts of molded, mass-produced, simulated ancient wrought iron. My focus shifted to my asshole, now being probed by Jim's tongue. He handed me poppers. I took several long breaths, alternating nostrils. The K had another effect it does sometimes, relaxing me, making me more easily persuaded, and hypertactile. Several more bumps of K and another hit of poppers. Jim's tongue returned to my ass. He seemed intrigued. I didn't mind—it felt intense—and I simply closed my eyes, no longer in the room. I could have been anywhere with anybody. After a couple of minutes, however, the poppers faded and I was back in a colorless room having my ass obsessed over by a punter. Luckily, another wave of K arrived; I stared at the ceiling and thanked God for drugs.

I assume more time passed in this way, with me listening to the sounds the mattress made or staring out the window at gray clouds merging against black sky into shapes, objects, faces. I recognized a photograph of myself at sixteen. I switched places with the clouds, became the photo, watching myself, what I was doing with Jim on the bed. *Remember who you are,* said sixteen-year-old Aiden.

Confusion. What was I doing? The sex I was having seemed almost real, definitely enjoyable. Was I cheating on Luke? Surely this shouldn't be part of a healthy relationship.

Focusing as well as I was able, I willed myself to stop tripping, to end this situation, my only job now to make Jim cum. It wasn't difficult; Jim seemed to be of the same mind. Knowing it would intensify his orgasm, he took a particularly big hit of poppers. A couple of minutes later—about thirty pounding strokes on his dick in cum time—he started to squirt, simultaneously reaching octopus-like for a pile of tissues and placing them exactly under his landing cum. Considering he was fucked up on poppers and K, I was impressed by his timing, agility, and coordination.

I waited what I thought the appropriate amount of time, then said, "Can I use the bathroom?"

"Yeah, it's just in there." He pointed to what I'd thought was a closet.

Feeling a little superfluous now he'd cum, I stepped off the bed and for the first time felt the carpet against my bare skin. I cringed, quickly put my socks on, and disappeared into the bathroom, where I couldn't help noticing that the carpet continued. Its glaring unobtrusiveness aggravated me. But there was no escape. I went in, closed the door, and found myself surrounded by dark blue walls and a blue bathroom suite—an oasis of color. A pink mat beside the bath made me think of *The Simpsons.*

I hitched my bum up over the side of the sink to wash off Jim's saliva and ran the hot tap water. On the tank of the toilet, opposite me, was a mirror, too low to see into when standing (when sitting you'd be facing away from it), but at the perfect height and position to see into when washing your bum. I felt ridiculous. Then I noticed how muscular my thighs looked, squashed against the sink, and how they complemented its blue color.

The water got too hot. I put in the plug, turned on both taps, washed my bum and dick thoroughly with antibacterial soap, and dried myself. I decided to try to pee. My dick was still a little too full of blood, but I stood waiting anyway. Then it dawned on me what the mirror was for. A few drops came out; I waited a little longer, encouraged. I knew from experience the best way to pee was to distract myself. I looked to my right. Through a shower curtain, transparent but for photographic starfish, sea horses, and coral, I could see skin products displayed as ornaments, arranged according to size and shape, perhaps even color. I gave up trying to pee and returned to the bedroom.

"Everything okay?" said the man.

"Yeah. Bright mat!"

"A present from my mother. She was here today."

"Oh," I said, thinking *how sweet* but also *how depressing*. I started to dress.

"You off then?" he said.

"I guess so."

"Do you want another drink?"

"No, thanks."

"That was fun."

"Yeah."

"Can I call you again?"

"Sure."

By the time I got home it was late. Luke was asleep, the apartment quiet and dark.

Wearing only a towel, I headed for the bathroom to shower properly and prepare for bed. A crack of light shone from under the door to Nina's room; hearing her voice, I knocked. The door opened slowly, sort of shakily, as if by someone old or frail. Nina stood like a startled fawn, silent and motionless on one foot, naked.

"Sorry," I said, and began to close the door.

"No, Aiden. Wait."

"Are you sure?"

"Yeah."

"Have I really interrupted something?"

"We were just getting down to it," she said.

"What? I mean, who?"

"Ching."

"Really! Where is she?"

"In the bathroom. You scared her."

"Sorry."

"It's okay."

Ching came in, also naked.

"Hello," I said. "Sorry for crashing in."

"It's no biggy," she said. "Shall we show you what we were doing?"

"Yes, please," I said.

"Sit down," said Ching.

I did as I was told.

"Face that way." She pointed at the far wall, then scuttled behind me. Opening her legs around my hips, she sang "One two three and bump," pushing her cunt against my back.

An unrecognizable sensation: the texture of pubic hair; something left behind, cooling and then drying. I couldn't help wondering what it felt like against another cunt.

Remains of some drug lay on a mirror beside the bed, along with some discarded-looking pages.

"Who's been writing?" I said.

"Me," said Nina.

"Anything interesting?"

"I hope so," she said. "I wrote it while Ching was licking my pussy. It's just my thoughts. Do you want to hear it?"

"Go for it."

"'Ancient shells. Ocean bed. Comfort. Open. Waves. Dreaming. Gliding. Floating. Flying.'" She paused, glanced at Ching, then at me. I got the feeling maybe she'd lost confidence in what she was reading. "What do you think?" she said, grinding her jaw.

"It sounds like it felt good."

"That sounds like a put-down."

"I'd never put you down. Well, not so you'd notice."

"Bastard!"

"No, seriously, you'll probably be glad you documented it. Sorry again for interrupting."

"Don't be silly," she said; then, to Ching (referring to where she sat and what she'd been doing): "May I?"

"He's all yours," said Ching and got up to make way.

Nina sang the same tune as Ching, but her bump was much more forceful.

"Hey, that's my boyfriend," said Luke in the doorway, smiling. "I'm the only one allowed to do that."

"I'd like to see you try," said Ching.

"Ha, ha," said Luke. "Clever dick."

"I don't think so," said Ching.

"Clever *cunt*," said Nina. "Listen, it's my last night. I'd like to make the most of it. Shall we go for a drink?"

"It's your night, baby," I said.

"How about a game of pool?" said Ching.

We headed to a place on Washington Avenue that was like a family version of a sleazy pool hall. A couple of sporty-looking boys sidled up to us at the bar, presumably interested in Nina and Ching, who, realizing this, immediately acted dykey—which in turn excited the boys.

"Aiden," said Nina, "can you get me a drink?"

"I'll get it," said the fair-haired boy, who looked like a mix of all the Waltons, including the girls.

"No, thanks."

"Why won't you let a guy get you a drink?" he protested.

"You wouldn't know what to get."

"You could tell me."

"I was going to let Aiden decide."

"What's so special about Aiden?"

"I don't know. I can't quite put my finger on it."

"Do you fancy a game of pool?" Ching asked the boys.

"Don't you want to play your friends?" said the shorter, darker, altogether sweeter-seeming boy.

"Let's play them," said the fair-haired boy. "My name's Brad, and this here's Rick."

"Well, what are you waiting for Brad, rack 'em up."

"Sure thing, ma'am."

I stayed at the bar, happy to be by myself, as they headed off. After a couple of shots of vodka chased with beer, I turned to see what they were up to.

Brad was bent over the table, taking his shot. His T-shirt had ridden up, revealing his back, the side of his brown stomach, and the top of white underwear. I walked toward them, intending to kiss Luke, who was staring at Brad's ass. I went to Nina and gave her the drink I'd got her. My face must have shown some confusion or upset, because she put her cheek against my chest and began panting like a puppy. Then she handed Rick her pool stick and did a handstand. I knew what to do next.

I lifted Nina by the ankles and hooked her legs over my shoulders. Her skirt fell over her head, revealing her underwear. Brad whistled. Using her stomach muscles, Nina pulled herself up until she sat with her legs around my neck, her cunt pressed against my face. Raising her arms like a trapeze artist, she bent down, pressed her mouth close to my ear, and said, "*I love you. Luke's a fool.*" Then, in a diving motion she slid over my shoulder and climbed down my body. When she reached the floor she stood on her hands for a moment, took a few steps, let her legs fall backward onto the floor, stood up—then dusted her hands off, reached for her pool stick, and potted two balls with one shot.

"Go girl!" said Ching, lifting her hand to receive a high five from Nina. They were winning.

"I want more drugs," said Ching.

"Hear, hear," said Nina.

"Your friend's a bit crazy," Rick said to me.

"Barely enough," I said.

"So?" said Ching.

"We've got no more money," said Nina.

"Don't worry," I said. "Some bloke just gave me a pile."

"Yes! Let's get some charlie," said Ching. Then, as though inspired: "An *eight ball.*"

"No," said Nina. "We can't spend all Aiden's money on coke. He had to have sex for that."

I looked at Luke. "I don't know if you could call it sex."

Brad and Rick appeared nervous. "We're probably going to move on," said Brad.

"Don't you want to get high?" said Ching.

"No, thanks," said Rick. "We really should be getting home."

They backed out as they spoke, disappearing through the entrance.

"An eight ball, then?" said Ching.

"Okay," I said. "Nina?"

"Yeah. If you're sure."

"Making you happy makes me happy," I said.

"That's my kind of guy," said Ching, and reached into my pocket for money. I liked her for doing this.

She was gone about ten minutes, and returned with lots of cocaine. Soon the night became little more than drinking, snorting, and wanting, until I was too fucked up to notice much at all, let alone that I'd spent everything I'd earned with Jim.

10

It rained nonstop for the next few days. We were all housebound. When it's not sunny in Miami, there's little to do.

Tristan called and booked me again, but still there was no work for Luke. Liam picked me up. He'd done some crystal before leaving his apartment and was very talkative.

"I had to," he said. "I've been up all night."

"Why?"

"Just having fun."

I gave him an exaggerated look of disapproval.

"Shucks, Aiden! You care."

"Probably." Before he had time to respond I said, "Slow down. The road's wet."

Liam sighed dramatically, like a child, but slowed down. We headed toward Fort Lauderdale. I leaned my face on the side window, losing myself in the passing colors and shapes: skyscrapers surrounded by car parks, roads, and low buildings, all separated from the freeway by great distance.

"Let me in," said Liam.

"It's not that interesting."

"Still, I'd like to."

"Okay, you're in."

"Am I?"

"To a certain extent."

"Listen, I've got a plan." He put on a Brooklyn accent. "I got family. Do you know what I mean?"

"I get it. You're connected."

"You're hearing me. I could have him dealt with."

"Who?"

"Luke. I could get rid of him."

I burst out laughing. "That's sweet of you, but . . . "

"It's nothing. I'm owed some favors." He paused a moment, squinting his eyes. "You know he's not right for you, don't you?"

"Maybe."

"If you were my boyfriend, I'd never let you do this work. I'd want you all to myself."

"That's how I felt a few weeks ago. This may sound stupid, but I think I'm doing it to make myself harder."

"Why would you want to be harder?"

"So I'm not destroyed."

"Aiden, you're bigger than that."

"How do you know?"

"You're trashing yourself. And because of *him*?"

"Maybe. But would you want me to give up, if we were boyfriends?"

"No."

"Relationships are complex."

"I know," he said, "but you're meant to be happy at least some of the time."

"I think the next turning is ours."

Liam switched on the internal overhead light so I could see the directions Tristan had given me. I looked up to tell Liam what I'd read, and for a moment we simply gazed at each other. I wanted to kiss him.

"You'll think I'm crazy, Aiden, but I love you."

He switched the light off and left me watching his profile. We drove in silence for a while, then he put the radio on. I turned it off.

"I'd rather listen to you," I said.

"My crystal babble?"

"Yeah. You remind me of what I wanted before I met Luke."

"Please don't change. You're right; he's wrong. Do what I say. Get rid of him."

Finally, he smiled.

The directions led us to a badly lit area of what looked like rundown army barracks. As instructed, we drove up the gravel path.

"This place is creepy," said Liam.

"You're telling me."

"Let's just leave. You don't need the money." Liam started to pull back.

A figure stepped from the doorway to one of the cabins, silhouetted by light. He appeared to be holding something.

"It's an alien," said Liam.

"Are you saying this might be interesting?"

"I'll put the headlights on full."

A young, scruffily dressed man stood stroking what looked like a dachshund.

"He's even creepier than I thought," said Liam. "Don't do it."

"Let me talk to him."

Liam pulled in front of the doorway. I stepped out.

"Are you Lez?"

"You found it," he mumbled, then said something I couldn't make out.

"It's a strange spot," I said, hoping to engage him in conversation and thereby figure him out. He didn't answer. I decided I'd go inside with him and see what happened.

I leaned my head into the car. "It should be all right."

Lez came up behind me. "Is this your driver?"

"That's right." I turned my head. "His name's Liam."

"Tell him to come back in half an hour."

"Is that enough time?" I said, wondering how long it took to be murdered.

The man mumbled something and walked toward his cabin. I gathered I was to follow.

"Don't worry," I told Liam. "Just come back in half an hour."

"Will you be okay?"

"Your guess is as good as mine."

The cabin was smaller inside than it had appeared from outside. I stood checking out the place, a grubby studio combining living and sleeping areas in one room. Everything smelled of dog.

Lez closed the door and wedged a book into the handle so it couldn't be opened from outside. I felt like something bad was going to happen.

"I know this place isn't very nice," Lez said, probably sensing my apprehension. He laughed nervously. "I was in a car crash today."

"Are you all right?" I said, scanning the room for doors that could possibly conceal somebody.

"My boyfriend might come back—hence the book in the door. I've got something you might find interesting."

He switched on the television. A porn video played. It looked familiar. At first I put this down to them often looking alike, then I recognized one of the models, Cliff Parker. I was the other. It was a video we'd done for Chi Chi LaRue. It brought back memories of endless sun and dim-witted LA party boys lying by swimming pools. My hair was peculiar, my body more so, not at all how I think it looks. This was probably due to my being so much younger—I was twenty-something and undeveloped—rather than because of my Body Image Disorder Syndrome.

I dragged myself back to the present—Lez, the room, the dog, dirt. "Can I use the toilet?" I said.

The bathroom was filthy and warm, the shower curtain closed around the tub. I pulled it open. The tub was full of dirty water. (I've yet to find a killer hiding in a bath, but I check anyway.) I flushed the toilet and hesitated. If I were attacked, what would I do? I went back into the other room, where Lez stood waiting, attentive, stroking the dog.

"Take your clothes off," he said.

"You, too," I said sexily, as though I meant it, not like I wanted to make sure he had no concealed weapons.

Feeling vulnerable, I undressed. Lez pulled down his sweatpants, wriggled and stepped out of them without letting go of the dog. The tops of his legs were hairless and wide. He walked toward me.

"Do you want to lose the dog?" I said.

"I'll, uh, put her in the bathroom."

The dog started scratching as soon as he closed the door, but Lez returned to the bed. "Shall we?" he said, referring to the dirty bed cover. We lay down.

He darted for my dick, pushed it around in his mouth. My eyes surveyed the room. The dog whined, Lez slurped, and my dick didn't get hard.

The phone rang. Lez picked it up and handed it to me.

"Are you okay?" said Liam.

I wanted to tell him to come get me. At the same time, I wanted to reassure him. But I wasn't sure myself. "Yeah, fine," I said. Lez looked uneasy. "I'll see you in half an hour." I hung up. A couple of minutes later, seemingly disconnected from my mind, my dick finally began got hard.

Lez stopped sucking and jumped to his feet. "This isn't going to work," he said.

"I was beginning to enjoy it," I lied.

"The dog. You're nervous. I'm nervous. This place. You weren't going to come in, were you?"

"My driver's very protective."

"Is he your boyfriend?"

I paused, for myself rather than effect. "No."

"Let's go to a hotel."

"How will my driver know where I am?"

"We'll come back."

"I'm sorry, I can't. There's not enough time."

"We could go somewhere nice. It wouldn't take long."

Again I lied. "I'm fine here."

"The dog's really annoying me," Lez said.

"Let it out of the bathroom."

"She'll jump on us, get in the way."

"What now, then?"

"My boyfriend might be home soon," he said. "Does that blow your mind?"

"It's an addition."

"Am I the weirdest customer you've ever had?" He laughed.

I didn't answer. I got off the bed, put on my boxer shorts, and moved to the sofa to put on my jeans. Lez disappeared into the kitchen.

"I haven't even got anything for you to drink," he said, returning with an empty bottle. "Look."

He collected the dog from the bathroom with one hand, holding the bottle with the other, and stood over me, a little too close for comfort, muttering the logistics of our situation—staying or going, what each might entail. He absentmindedly pushed the dog's paw into the neck of the bottle.

My eyes must have widened.

"Have I blown your mind?" he said.

"Is that the intention?"

"Not really."

I pictured him hitting me with the bottle.

"What shall we do?" he said.

"Well, I've got to pay the driver and the agency."

"Don't worry. Don't get me wrong, you're everything they said you were. But this isn't working."

"We could try again another time."

"But I'd, uh, you know, like to get fucked."

"Did the agency say I'd do that?"

"Not really."

"We're running out of time." I finished dressing. "Shall I just go?"

"Okay."

I got up and stood by the door. "Can I see if my driver's here?"

"Go ahead."

I removed the book that jammed the handle, and went outside. Liam was there, waiting. Lez was rummaging around a kitchen drawer as I came back in. "I've got something for you," he said, chuckling. I stood in the doorway, ready to slip out rapidly if necessary. My eyes darted from the waiting car to Lez, who was far enough away not to worry me too much.

"Your money," he said, pulling a bunch of fifty-dollar bills from the drawer.

"Thanks. That's kind of you."

I made my exit just slowly enough to be polite, got in the car, and shut the door. Lez stood in the entryway to his funny little cabin, watching.

"Quick, let's get out of here," I whispered urgently to Liam, hoping Lez couldn't read lips.

"What the fuck!"

"I'll tell you in a minute."

We drove off.

"I got you a beer, but mind you don't let the cops see you drinking it."

"Right," I said, remembering I was in America and subject to its laws. I opened the beer and finished it off before we were out of the barrackslike area.

Liam pulled over. "Aiden, you're scaring me. What happened?"

"Nothing. He was just a bit creepy."

"Duh! You shouldn't have done it."

"Don't worry. I'm okay."

"What happened?"

"Nothing!"

"I'm not doing this again."

"You're sweet."

"I mean it. That could have been dangerous. I don't want to be part of this."

"Liam, I appreciate—"

He cut me off. "I don't like you doing this, and I don't mind saying so."

I stared ahead and drank another beer. My mind wandered.

"Aiden?"

"I'm here," I said, returning to the situation I was actually in.

"I don't understand why you're doing this."

"Neither do I."

"So stop."

I quickly finished two more beers and began to come round. "Can we go somewhere for dinner?" I said.

"Anywhere you like."

"How about Coconut Grove? The Cheesecake Factory does chicken and biscuits."

"I don't believe you Brits. Chicken and biscuits?"

"What's wrong with that? When in America . . ."

"Okay. Whatever you want."

My mood softened as we ate. Liam tried to seduce me, and to an extent succeeded. But I couldn't help thinking he wouldn't be interested in me if I didn't have a boyfriend. After dinner he dropped me at home. Luke was already sleeping. I got into bed carefully, so as not to wake him. He looked so lovely. I curled myself around him and kissed his neck. His smell was familiar, his shape comfortable.

The next morning I had breakfast with David, who was leaving for London that afternoon. We hadn't spent much time together since Luke had arrived in Miami.

"How are you?" I said.

"Okay. How are *you*?"

"Lonely, I think"

"Why?" said David. "You've got Luke."

"Do you think?"

"I *had* wondered," said David. "Let's see how you feel about it when you get home."

"Yeah, it may be different with him not around."

"Easier to believe he's your boyfriend?"

"Maybe."

"Virtual boyfriends *are* easier than actual ones."

"I hope so."

11

Luke and I were sitting on a bench on Washington Avenue outside an ice cream bar when his beeper went off. We headed to a pay phone, where Luke called Tristan back. Hanging up, he looked confused and annoyed.

"He's so high he can hardly speak. No wonder I never get any work."

"What did he want?" I said.

"He's invited us to a sex party, with two other guys."

We headed home. Within seconds, Luke got another page, from a number he didn't recognize. He called the number and spoke to Rod, one of the guys having the sex party (Tristan had given them our number). After Luke had answered question after question in his porn-star voice, Rod asked to speak to me. He was persistent. I told him Luke and I would get back to him.

Luke was keen on the idea. We rode over on our bikes. Before we rang the bell, Rod was at the door, wearing only shorts. I didn't find him attractive. His nose looked altered and he had that wizened South Beach look, part beef jerky and part melting toffee, probably due to the unmerciful cocktail of crystal and sun. The front door led directly into the living room of the small apartment; porn played on a huge TV screen, with techno music from a stereo as the soundtrack (all those sex noises directors had asked me to make would have been wasted here). The sofas and armchairs were covered in sheets, with a double-ended dildo and some lube on what looked like a sofa.

Rod offered us GHB, cocaine, and K. There was no alcohol in the house, since it was believed to be dangerous if mixed with G. But alcohol seemed to make the G work better for me, so I'd brought along beer. Having a rough idea what was required of me physically and emotionally, I went into my I-can-be-anything-I-have-to-be mode, and was able to put up enough of a façade that nobody appeared to notice it was contrived.

"We heard there was a sex party here," I said. "Have we missed it?"

"No, we're just taking a break. I see you're the more forward of the two," said Rod.

"Do you think?" I said.

No one spoke for a minute or two. It felt like longer. We sat awkwardly on the covered sofa, Rod on my right, Luke on my left.

"Where's the boyfriend?"

"Gone to get more lube," said Rod, looking relieved that he had something to say.

"Then I guess it's your job to entertain us until he comes back. Show us the goods," I said.

"You first," he said, feigning shyness.

"Oh, come on."

"Okay," said Rod, jumping to his feet, "but you have to do the same."

He went to the middle of the room, facing away from Luke and me, the porn on the TV casting him into a pretty, almost sexy silhouette.

Pulling down his shorts, he bent over and came up as though to applause, turned around, and fiddled self-consciously with his dick.

"It's the crystal," he explained.

Luke stood up, rubbing his abdomen and peeling off his shirt, simultaneously sliding his hand over his crotch, in character. He went to Rod, swank in his walk. He pouted and fluttered his eyelashes, seductively unzipped and lowered his jeans. Rod loved it, but I had to stop myself from laughing.

"Your turn, baby," he said with his porn voice, still in his own world.

I stood in place, removed my T-shirt, dropped my jeans. Then I replaced them, telling myself I was too cool to do this silly performance, whereas the truth was I was bitter, angry, resentful, and deeply confused by the situation.

Rod paged his boyfriend, who arrived within five minutes.

Alex had streaked hair and an even darker tan than Rod. He shook our hands; apparently etiquette at a sex party was important to him. With him stood a pretty, altogether different sort of man.

"Who's this?" I said.

"Guido," said Alex.

Guido put his hand up in greeting and said, "Hi." He seemed refined, a severe contrast to Alex's cheesy persona. I gestured for him to sit next to me on the sofa while the others began touching, rubbing, and kissing behind us.

"My name's Aiden," I said.

"I know who you are."

"That's not to be confused with knowing me."

"I'm not stupid," he said.

"What are you doing here, then?"

He glanced at the others, then back at me. "Looking for love," he said.

I was surprised—and pleased. We continued to talk while Rod and Alex and Luke continued whatever they were doing; I heard sucking, underwear elastic snapping against skin, and the occasional, "Ooh, yeah!" but didn't want to look. Gradually, they engulfed Guido and me.

It was frantic—so many limbs and too many personalities—but Luke looked happy. Unable to relax, to be anything I had to be, I took a lot of drugs.

Hard as it was for me to play this part mentally, physically it was familiar. It was like every other time I'd had sex with a group of men, only this time I didn't want to be there. Maybe I just didn't fancy the group enough.

Luckily the drugs ran out, which meant somebody had to go for more. I volunteered, wanting to get out of the apartment, away from the gnarled sex. Guido offered to drive. Luke preferred to stay; as I left, I remember hoping he'd have fun. I must have been really high.

Guido's Jeep had no roof. He sang along to a CD mixed by some club DJ. He seemed higher than me at this point and drove accordingly. We came to an abrupt stop outside the building where Liam and Jim lived. Guido jumped out of the Jeep as if he were in a cop movie.

The dealer's apartment was David Lynch with a gay sexual slant. We got the gear and did some cocaine, promising to return later (knowing we wouldn't).

Back in Rod and Alex's living room, Guido and I found discarded dildos and lube. They'd probably tried fucking and had to resort to dildos because nobody could get hard. I told myself I was too high to care. The action had moved to the bedroom.

Another round started. Rod and Alex didn't interest me in the slightest, and having sex with Luke felt odd, not the same as when we were alone. This left Guido. I tried to focus, but there were too many big men on too small a bed, too much noise, hair, and suntanned skin.

The mattress was in constant motion, which made us lose balance, miss targets, and generally act clumsier than we ordinarily would have when fucked up. I found it impossible to concentrate. Apart from the video (which I knew was staged), I didn't see a hard dick the whole time, including my own. I needed to get away from the dazed bodies on the bed.

I went into the bathroom and locked the door. Why didn't I just leave? I was too high—where would I go? And maybe something about the scenario made me want to be part of it.

The K was affecting my sight; wherever I focused, the point would fracture into ice crystals with coloring like petrol on water. I recognized the beginning of a K hole, only prettier, less consuming. I tried to pee, then remembered it had only been an excuse to escape. After what seemed like a plausible amount of time, I was standing at the bedroom door, thinking how clichéd and comical everyone looked.

I made my way back into the thick of it.

Guido gestured for me to go in the living room, where he asked me if Luke and I would like to come to his place after the sex party. I had no idea when that would be, but agreed. The longer I spent with Rod and Alex, the more grotesque I found them. By the time Guido, Luke, and I got out of their apartment, I'd come down so much that I'd changed my mind about going home with Guido. My feelings were raw. Nevertheless, a series of brittle movements brought us into Guido's Jeep, then his apartment, where we undressed yet again.

We lay on Guido's bed, Luke kissing him all over. I closed my eyes. Coming down from drugs, Luke and I having sex with somebody else didn't make sense to me. If I stopped taking drugs, this kind of thing might happen less, but Luke would still want sex with others. Being high made me more able to be there. Of course, I didn't have to be there, or be Luke's boyfriend, but these choices didn't feel like options. Wanting to communicate something of this to Luke, I watched him, hoping to catch his eye. Luke lay with his head near Guido's dick, stroking it, his eyes closed, a look of bliss on his face.

I glanced at Guido's bedside clock. It was ten A.M.

"Baby?"

Luke opened one eye and gave me his lazy smile. "Yeah, tulip?"

He had never called me this before.

"I've got to take my meds."

"Do you have them with you?"

"No. I'll have to go home." For a fraction of a second, I thought I might have to leave alone.

"Let's go, then. Do you mind, Guido?"

"No problem. Do you want me to come?"

"Sure," said Luke.

Guido looked at me for a response. "Are you sure it's okay?" he said.

He seemed so vulnerable. This made me not want to abandon him.

"Sure," I said.

Again I tried to catch Luke's eye, but he was already back at Guido's crotch and it was Guido who noticed. He made an expression; I couldn't tell what it meant.

At my apartment, I took my meds and we all took sleeping tablets. I woke up about four hours later with Luke behind me and Guido staring into my eyes. Luckily, he had to walk his dog. He looked so sad that he had to go home, I suggested we meet for dinner.

Once Guido was gone, I attempted to let Luke know how I felt, but the more I said, the more ridiculous I sounded to myself. Embarrassed, I gave up.

We were to meet Guido at a restaurant on Lincoln Mall. Luke and I got there first and sat at a table outside. Guido showed up on roller blades, in shorts.

"Nice legs," Luke said quietly to me.

"Hey!" said Guido.

Luke noticed my mood had changed. "What's wrong, baby? Drug fallout?"

"Maybe."

Guido sat next to me and rubbed my neck.

"That's nice," I said.

"I know," said Guido.

"Hey!" said Luke. "That's my job."

"Yeah, but I got there first," said Guido.

Luke went to the toilet. I looked at Guido, who smiled, making me do the same. It was nice getting to know a new person, especially one who seemed so sensitive. For a moment, the last twelve hours seemed worthwhile.

"This may be out of line," said Guido, "but I couldn't care less whether or not he was there."

"What do you mean? When?"

"Aiden. I didn't have sex with you both."

"What do you mean?"

"I had sex with you. He just happened to be there."

"I'm sorry."

"Don't apologize. You obviously love each other."

"You think?"

"Don't you?"

"I'm not happy," I said.

"Why?"

"I didn't enjoy last night." Guido looked hurt. "I think *you're* lovely, but if I hadn't had so many drugs, I couldn't have done it."

"You don't have to do it."

"I want to, well, be able to at least."

"Are you sure?"

"I'm confused. I thought I wanted monogamy, but it makes sense to be able to have an open relationship."

"I wouldn't want one."

"It seems nobody would," I said. "Except Luke."

"If it's not right for you . . ." He paused, looking into his lap.

"I thought I'd get used to it, in time."

"Maybe you will."

"I hope so, I think."

Luke returned to the table. "How are the two hottest boys in South Beach?"

"I'm hardly a boy," I said.

"I don't know," said Guido, squeezing my leg under the table.

12

Dusk was probably beautiful, but my senses were shrouded by dejection. Luke was playing volleyball on the beach with a group of men who met there every day. I was never invited, and assumed Luke didn't want me along. Instead of accepting that he needed time to himself, I felt resentful and jealous. Hoping at least to distract myself, I went for a ride on my bike.

Eight blocks from my apartment, the chain slipped. I pulled off the road to fix it, onto a patch of pavement lit by pale blue neon from a sign with large, swirling letters: MEDIUM. Then, smaller, as if to clarify: Cognitive Examinations. Ordinarily, I'd have smiled or rolled my eyes and got back on my bike, but suddenly it began to pour (such dramatic weather changes are common in Miami during December and January). I ran into the neon-lit doorway for shelter.

The rain splashed around my feet and wet the front of my T-shirt. I turned to the glass door, on the other side of which hung black lace curtains. Inside the room was a wicker chair painted glossy black, facing a low wicker table painted matte salmon, with tarot cards laid out in a fan. A tiny shelf on the wall held different-colored candles, a crucifix, and bones—an odd mix of witchcraft, Christianity, and voodoo. A woman stood by the window, watching me. She walked toward me with a cheeky smile, opened the door just a little, and said, "Come out of the rain."

The room smelled of incense and food. Each wall was papered with patterned flock painted over with tangy, glossy purple. A sprinkling of gold glitter covered the thick black pile carpet.

"Would you like a cup of coffee?" the woman said. "I was about to have one myself. It helps me focus."

"Yes, please," I said, then asked, "What is it that you do?"

"I can tell you things, give you advice about your lover."

"Could you tell me her name?"

"Come now. You trying to trick an old dear?"

"Sorry. His name?"

"Probably not." The woman grinned.

"What could you tell me, then?"

"We should sit and talk."

"How much does it cost?"

"Seeing as it's your first time, twenty dollars."

"That seems fair."

"It is." She clipped back a stray curl of her blonde wig. Her face was large, her makeup thin but for the vivid red blusher high on her cheekbones. A light dusting of gold glitter, the same as in the carpet, coated each eyelid.

"You having a tough time?" she asked.

"I think so," I said. Despite my skepticism, I found her comforting, like an optimistic horoscope.

"Take a seat. Let me get your coffee."

I stared through the curtained window at what I could make out of the street. Soon she was back, carrying two steaming cups.

"You seem like a sensitive man."

Was this going to be about flattering twenty dollars out of me? "Really?"

"And romantic."

"Sometimes." This seemed general.

"More than most," she continued, looking nowhere in particular, as though searching for the information, but I guessed just using her imagination.

"It seems that way."

"You cannot make him anything he's not."

She'd struck a chord.

"What do you mean?"

"You know what I mean."

I changed the subject. "What else can you tell me?"

"Things you might not want to hear."

"Like what?"

She shook her head as if to say she wouldn't tell me, then, finding something she would, said, "He's too young for your old soul."

Tired soul might have been more accurate. Still, I said, "How do you know that?"

"I don't *know*. I'm told."

I went to speak, but she silenced me with a gesture, smiling a smile that looked like it wasn't hers but could easily belong to someone who loved me. As though on autopilot, she took my hand and examined it thoroughly, rubbing it as though she were trying to get color in it, to bring it back to life.

"It will be okay," she said.

Sensing doubt in her voice, I said, "Just okay?"

"You're not the kind who wants to know everything, are you?"

I paused. "No?"

"Sometimes it's best that way."

"So, what am I doing here?"

The woman laughed. After a moment, she looked me in the eye for the first time since bringing in the coffee.

"You don't approve of him."

"I do!"

"Is that the truth?"

Embarrassed, again I opted for distraction.

"What's your name?" I said.

"Why don't you approve of him?"

"He wants an open relationship."

She nodded. "And you don't."

"I don't know any more."

"You should do nothing," she said gently.

"But I love him."

"Are you sure?"

"I think so."

"There's some of the problem."

"What, the love or my uncertainty?"

"Love's not the problem. It never is. It's what we load on top of it." Seeing me nodding, she continued. "Expectations, jealousy, all sorts of unnecessary stuff."

The room seemed suddenly dingy. My eyes settled somewhere in my lap. A scrawny hand lifted my chin. I flinched. The fingers smelled of peanut butter.

"I've upset you," said the woman. She looked concerned.

"No. I mean, yes. But you're probably right."

"Finish your coffee." She watched me as I glanced around the room. "The name's Nova," she said, and burst into laughter.

"It's not that funny."

"But it is funny."

I heard something behind me. A very tall man stood in the doorway.

"Don't worry," Nova said to him. "We've finished here."

The man's mouth shaped into a smile. By the time I turned back to Nova, her expression had changed. She looked serious.

"There's something you should know."

"Something bad?"

Nova closed her eyes, nodded. I was spooked.

"What are you saying?"

"Be careful."

"Is it Luke?"

"No, he won't be there."

"That's out of order," I said.

"This whole thing is out of order."

Was this a device to make me come back? It seemed cruel to leave me hanging. Skeptical as I was, she got through, left me less sure of my opinions.

Nova stood, put her hands together, looked over my shoulder to the man behind me. Getting her attention, I handed her a twenty-dollar bill, then another five, having no idea how much to tip in this situation, or even if it was appropriate.

Nova lowered her head. I hoped her response was an old-fashioned, grand way of saying thank you. Then, with a hand on my arm as though for security, she guided me to the door. Although a bit weird, it felt right. She opened the door and said, "It's cleared up." I guessed she meant the rain had stopped; she couldn't have been referring to my thoughts or feelings.

In fact, the rain had stopped. Nova left my side. I looked back, but she seemed busy already with the man. I stepped onto the sidewalk. When the door was almost closed, Nova called after me.

"Bye, dear. Be careful."

13

January came to an end, and with it my winter break. Luke and I were leaving the same day. He woke me at five A.M. to say good-bye, reminding me that I'd promised to visit him in San Francisco. When I woke again, I called Liam and Guido to say good-bye. I couldn't get hold of Liam, but Guido wanted to meet me for breakfast.

It was a beautiful morning; I set off toward the Eleventh Street Diner, pedaling slowly to enjoy the bougainvillea-covered garden walls and palm trees lining the streets, so unlike London's. Geckos warming themselves on the pavement scurried to safety. I sped up; power surged through my limbs, invigorating warm air rushed past my face, under my arms, through my legs. Everything felt different. Some pressure had been lifted from me, and I sprang free.

I got to the diner before Guido and took in its Americanness, unsure how long it would be before I experienced it again. When Guido arrived, I ordered pancakes with maple syrup.

After breakfast we walked along the water. The world seemed less intense, less about men, sex, and Luke. I sat on the shore with Guido and gazed out at the ocean, taking in the sounds and smells and beauty that must have been there for the last two months, but which, in my infatuation, I'd been unaware of.

Guido took me to the airport, his driving as reckless as when he was high. When I asked him to slow down, he responded angrily, "Everyone's always complaining about my driving. If you don't like it, you can walk." By the time we reached my terminal, I was anxious to get out of the Jeep.

My flight to London was a redeye; with the help of tablets, I slept all the way.

I'd sublet my apartment, so I went from Heathrow to David's to stay with him for a few weeks—a nice change, especially since returning to an empty apartment always depressed me, and the two months spent with Luke had left me feeling trampled.

I tried willing myself to shut Luke out, picturing him having sex with other men, but my first night back I slept fitfully. When I got up to go to the toilet, I saw in the mirror the deeply creased frown on my forehead. I woke the next day feeling tender, like I'd always wanted to feel. I hated it.

Staying with David was a kind of hospice. He nurtured me with kindness and soft intelligence; spending time with him was like my right foot keeping company with my left. Without Luke around, I relaxed.

My first Saturday back, David and I decided to go to a club. Marc was supposed to come with us, but was still nursing the aftereffects of midweek smack. Nina had to rehearse the next morning with some other band for whom she played bass. I called a dealer in Islington to make sure he had what we wanted, then David drove me to pick it up. The journey took about an hour; by the time we got back to London, it was twelve-thirty. I put the cocaine into a little bottle in my pocket to protect it against getting wet from sweat at the club. The K went into bullets, one for each of us. There are two good things about bullets: you never confuse the drugs and wind up doing too much K, and bullets are easy to do at the bar or even on the dance floor. You don't have to trek to a toilet cubicle every time you want some.

We did two lines of cocaine and each had a beer from the fridge, then caught a cab to the club, where we checked our coats and headed for the bar. It was past one o'clock and the club was full of sweat-soaked men. David and I did some K and merged in the crowd. Men looked at us and we looked back. We became part of a group, losing then rejoining them. Two New Yorkers, wanting to go home with David, gave him Ecstasy. On a trip to the bar, he got hold of my arm, pulled me toward him, and said, "If I evaporate, will you breathe in?"

"Of course. I'd die otherwise," I said.

I left him dancing with the Americans and went upstairs to the toilet. The crowd looked uninspiring. I took off my T-shirt, handed it to a tall man, asked him to remove the single blue bulb that was the room's only light, and unbuttoned my jeans. Unseen hands grabbed at my dick until someone claimed it, sucking on it for a couple of minutes then standing and tugging me—an invitation to go into a cubicle. As we closed the door, someone slid in with us, offering us poppers like a VIP ticket (unnecessary: he would have been on the list anyway). I took some, felt the rush, and kissed him (it's a shame not to when you've had poppers). After minutes of soft dicks and awkward groping, I excused myself, blaming it on the drugs, edged through the men outside the cubicle, and made my way downstairs.

David was still with the relentless New Yorkers, who now were at the bar. Apparently they both wanted to fuck David. He was in the mood to be on top. Eventually we managed to shake them off and spent a little time in the downstairs toilet, where I went into cubicles with a couple of men but couldn't get into it. I stood on the dance floor feeling I had no personality, certainly no charisma, until Ben, a man we'd both known for some time, hooked up with us.

Outside the club, people waited with intent looks on their faces. I suggested we get somebody else; otherwise there would be an odd number. David spoke to a boy named Kurt, who agreed to make it a foursome. We haggled with a few iffy-looking unlicensed cabdrivers (it had less to do with the price they quoted than with their attitude).

Near Chelsea Bridge, flashing lights appeared behind us. (The strip of the Embankment from Battersea to Chelsea was notorious for police picking off clubbers. They often managed to book the unlicensed cab as well as its passengers—a real catch.) Luckily for me, I was in the middle of doing cocaine and K and therefore had the drugs out of my pocket. I tossed them under the driver's seat in front of me. Three policemen got out of their cars and surrounded ours (as much as you can with three people), shining their torches at us. The pupils of our eyes must have given away enough. Ben, David, and Kurt were told to get out to be searched. Waiting and watching for one of the policemen to become available, I noticed the white powder covering my black jeans. By the time it was my turn to be searched, I'd dusted off enough to be presentable. I stood with my arms outstretched and was frisked.

The police arrested David and placed him in custody.

"Where's he being taken?" I asked my officer.

"Chelsea police station."

"Why?" I acted surprised.

"We believe we found cocaine on him."

"Really?" Now I *was* surprised; I'd been looking after the coke. "Can he be contacted?"

"He'll probably call you. Otherwise, you can phone the station."

"How long will he be kept?"

"A couple of hours. Do you have anything on you we should know about?"

"Sleeping tablets."

"Prescription?"

"Yep."

"What kind?"

"Rohypnol." I couldn't help feeling a little proud, as they were getting increasingly hard to obtain.

"I've heard of them."

"Right! There's been enough fuss about them, people calling them the date-rape drug."

"Maybe I should try some," he said, I think meaning to be funny and seem human.

Before long I rejoined Ben in the taxi. Kurt, too, was eventually let go, and we set off. I retrieved my drugs from under the driver's seat and did more of each.

At David's we shared a joint, had a drink, and I fucked Ben and Kurt. David telephoned to let me know he was okay and would be home soon.

"Save some for me," he said.

"What, sex?"

"No."

"Don't worry, there's plenty left."

"Good."

"Are you sure you're okay?" I said.

"Yes. It's quite interesting, really."

"Freak. I'm sorry, but I've got to go. I'm busy."

"I can tell you love me," he said.

We both laughed.

Sex on drugs can seem never-ending; after twenty minutes of fucking, I got bored. In situations like this, cumming often serves as punctuation, rounding things off, so I warned Ben. He asked if I'd cum inside him. I trusted he was making an informed decision (he was a doctor and knew I was positive). Once we'd both cum, I went to wash my dick. It was covered in a thin, even layer of shit. When I got back, Ben and Kurt were smoking a joint and talking. I lay down, closed my eyes, and listened to them. Kurt went to wait in David's bed.

Suddenly I couldn't bear to be awake. I took three sleeping tablets, wishing Ben and Kurt would leave.

Facing me, Ben became affectionate, as though we were on intimate footing. His breath, his skin, the heat of his body repelled me. I begged myself to fall asleep, the word *please* repeating in my head.

Sensing something wrong, Ben said, "Are you okay?"

"No," I said, and began to cry.

I kept crying until I fell asleep.

14

Reluctantly, I moved back into my apartment. Nothing was where I'd left it. Cups and plates were broken. Cutlery was missing, as well as a pillow from my bed and two slipcovers. The more I noticed, the more I hated the person who'd done this. I decided never to let out my home again.

I joined an escort agency called Jerry's, meaning to recoup my over-spending in Miami. I was miserable. My sex drive was low; it took a lot of effort to conjure up a hard-on with punters. Sometimes, when alone, I reminisced about Luke, the bliss I'd sometimes, if rarely, experienced when wrapped around him. I missed him—or, rather, what I wanted him to be.

Marc called and asked me to meet him for lunch at a café in Soho.

I'd first met Marc at art college in Brighton. He'd come bounding out of the entrance with rolled-up paper under one arm, a battered portfolio under the other, and a mass of lilac-colored dreadlocks. The next time I saw him was in a local gay club. Drink in hand, I went up to him and said, "You go to my college, don't you?"

"No," he replied, "you go to mine."

We continued to talk, and collaborated on art pieces and performances. More than friends, we were allies—against college tutors, society, anybody we saw as moralistic. We wanted to have an effect, to change things. Thinking it nonconformist and rebellious, we decided to become sex workers.

This was before there were gay magazines with escort ads, and Brighton wasn't a large city with well-frequented cruising areas (apart from public toilets). Nor did we want to walk the streets. We made up false names, photographed ourselves in sexy, nonpornographic poses, and designed and printed "business cards" (using Letraset, a forerunner of computer graphics, courtesy of the college.) These we posted in all the local establishments where gay men were likely to see them—pubs, clubs, guesthouses, hotels, saunas.

Our little self-promotion campaign worked, and so did we (we were quite popular as a double act). We even used it in our college artwork. We might do contemporary/new dances to a text by Genet, squalid pieces full of lust, frustration, and violence, or I might write the text, at times romantic, loaded with longing, at other times brutal and raw. A naturally accomplished dancer, Marc would perform pieces we worked on together, or improvise a strange mix of exactness and creative abandon. After finishing college we moved to London, where the sex industry was better organized and more sophisticated, and for the rest of our early twenties we worked in a Mayfair brothel. We made a lot of money and spent most of it on drugs.

Ten years later, Marc was still one of my closest friends. I'd seen him in many different states, often coming down off something, rarely truly happy, and (for a while in the late 1980s) near death due to AIDS, until meds revived him. The dreadlocks had been cut off shortly after I met him. Now his hair was casually pushed back, handsome and stylish— and dyed blue, which suited his skin tone so well that somehow it looked natural.

"Hair's cute," I said. "How's the therapy going?"

"Thanks. It seems a bit superficial."

"Your hair?"

"No, therapy."

"Why don't you change therapists?"

"What good would that do?"

"You might find someone who'll fix you."

"I can't see how. It's not as though they can change me."

"Would you like to change?"

"Um!" he said, nodding sincerely.

"What?"

"You name it."

"I wouldn't change a blue hair on your head."

"What about the gray ones? I can't see the point in life."

"They might be able to change that."

"I can't see how."

"That's probably because you're depressed. Have you tried antidepressants?"

"Yeah. I couldn't stand the feeling."

"And you like the way you feel now? How long did you take them? Apparently, they settle down after a while."

"Three weeks. I couldn't wait."

"So curl up and die," I said.

"It's not that easy."

"I know. Do you want some cake? It's chocolate."

"Immediate gratification isn't the answer," he said, as though reading from a textbook.

"I don't think you heard me. It's chocolate."

"Okay!" he squealed.

I laughed and tried to tickle his ribs.

"I'd happily have ten minutes under the covers with someone I love, then die," he continued. "That, or a lifetime of misery. I can't decide."

I was angry and upset when Marc left me. I wasn't the best person to justify living. Most of the time, I couldn't see the point myself. Having someone around who was more depressed sometimes made me feel better, but today I was more porous than usual. Negativity invaded.

As soon as I got home, Jerry's called, with an appointment in two hours. I had a bath and got ready, feeling anxious. Jerry's insisted that their escorts wear suits when seeing clients. I thought this pretentious, even a bit ridiculous, but I also liked it. It was the only time I ever dressed so smartly.

The punter's flat was on Bond Street, above a clothes shop. I rang the bell. To my surprise, a pleasant face greeted me. Eduardo was Brazilian. Well-kempt and clean, he was suntanned and a little overweight, which made him look quite cute. He wore perfume, but not so much that I'd smell of it after washing. Apparently, he was a successful photographer. He showed me pictures he'd taken in the Valley of the Kings, mostly of Egyptian tombs and pyramids.

Eduardo was a happy man who seemed to like making others happy. He flattered me from beginning to end, making me more pleasant company, a better prostitute. I couldn't help smiling as I lay on my back and he knelt between my legs, rubbing my abdomen. I felt like his pet. He asked if I'd visit him in Paris. I gave him my telephone number—something the agency frowned upon—and left in a better mood than I'd arrived in.

In the cab home I zoned out, staring into space—my reaction to doing a punter even when the experience was pleasant; I wondered if I was using tried-and-true methods to help me detach from Luke. Why was it necessary to protect myself from him?

I spent the following evening watching TV. Before bed, I telephoned Luke.

"Baby!"

"Hey, Rufus, when you coming to San Fran?"

"I don't think I will."

"Why?"

"I'm not happy with our relationship."

"Why?"

"I think we want different things."

"Does that mean you're giving up?"

"It means I don't have confidence in you."

"Would you like me to come to London?"

"Maybe."

"If that's what I have to do to prove I love you, I'll do it."

"That's very sweet."

"So suck me. You know you'd like to."

"Ha, ha."

"I'll get a flight in a couple of weeks. It will be cheaper then."

"Can you afford it?"

"Yeah. I've been working loads."

"What were you doing before I called?"

"Painting the bathroom."

"What color?"

"I'm doing it like your living room."

"Ah. Home from home?"

"It's so hot in here."

"Why don't you take off your T-shirt?"

"I'm only wearing boxer shorts."

"I bet you look beautiful," I said.

"Baby's horny?"

"I wasn't. But now I'm getting a chubby."

"You mean a woody. It's always chubby."

"Lately it's been kind of a nonevent."

"My baby a nonevent? I don't think so."

"Really. I haven't felt like using it."

"How about now?"

"On the phone? No."

"Why?"

"It's silly."

"You're silly. Why not?"

"I don't know."

"Go get a towel."

"I can use my T-shirt."

"Are you ready?"

"As ready as I'll ever be."

"Just stroke your dick and picture me," Luke said. I was pleased that he didn't switch to his porn voice. "Have you got me in your head?"

"Yes."

"Okay. We're both naked. I'm pushing my dick between your legs."

"Stop, you're hurting me."

"I haven't even put it in yet."

"Is it too late to change positions?"

"If that's what you want. Picture me bent over the sink."

"Can't we go in your bedroom? It's not as comfortable, standing up."

"Comfortable for who?"

"Sorry, baby."

"Okay, just for you—I know this is your favorite. We're in bed. The covers are pulled over our heads. Are you with me?"

"Right next to you."

I jerked my dick. Ordinarily when wanking, many chaotic sexual images flashed in and out of my mind, but not now with Luke on the phone.

"How do you feel, baby?" he said.

"You tell me, you're next to me."

"You feel perfect."

"You, too."

After little coaxing, I was already close to cumming.

As though he really was inside my head and knew what I was feeling and thinking, he said, "Are you close?" Right on cue.

"Yeah," I said.

"I'm ready when you are."

The thought of Luke cumming got me closer. "Same, same, baby."

"Okay, I'm going to cum. I love you, baby."

This sent me over the edge. "Me too, baby. I love you."

"Stay on the phone, baby," he said. "I want to hear you cum." His voice sounded different; I assumed he was cumming.

"I'm cumming, baby," I said.

"Go on, baby. I love you."

"Jesus! Jesus!" I came.

We were silent a moment. Our breathing slowly returned to normal.

"Where did you cum?" I said.

"On the floor. What about you?"

"On my stomach."

"I'd love to lick it off."

"If it meant you being here to sleep with, I'd like that, too."

We rounded off the conversation with more cooing, and finally said good night. I went to bed satisfied, as though I'd had good sex.

15

Luke let himself in while I was pottering around my desk—I'd given him the key the last time he'd visited—and came toward me. His hair was bleached almost white. With an expression I found familiar but had never really understood, he reached for me, took hold of me, hugged me. But the way he held me felt different, and he looked at the floor, not at me. He's traveled a long way to be with me, I told myself. He loves me. I will try hard to make it work between us. As if he knew I was convincing myself of something, Luke took my hand and led me into the bedroom.

The scent of hyacinths saturated the room. I'd frosted the windows for privacy and to make the light softer. The air looked as though it had been powdered. Luke's hair, his eyes and teeth, the duvet, the sheets—everything seemed to glow white. My bedroom felt magical. Our transition into bed was seamless, yet once under the sheets I was strangely self-conscious about being naked. We held each other, kissed. My mind quieted. As we had sex, I began to believe in Luke, be in love with him again.

I would have been content staying at home and doing nothing but appreciating Luke, but he had a list of places he wanted to see in the week we had together. And I wanted to show him as much of the city as possible. I tried to make every moment count. We went to the British Museum and the Tate, bought gifts for his friends, and searched for shot glasses for his mum.

The evening before he was to leave, we walked around Covent Garden and the West End, down through Piccadilly Circus to the steps leading from Pall Mall where we stopped to look at statues, then crossed into St. James's Park. With every step we took, the city dispersed more and stillness enveloped us. The air was cleaner. The park was picturesque, the edges of each tree and branch defined in moonlight, a whole new spectrum of color: muted beige, deep greens, glowing yellows.

Luke and I gazed at each other.

"I love you so much," I said.

"I love you as well," he responded.

"You called me by my real name."

"What?"

"Aswell."

"Only because you finally called me by my real name, Somuch."

Luke's hand was warm in mine. We continued walking. The path wound deeper. I lifted my face to his and we stopped to kiss.

"Will you be okay?" Luke said.

"I think so."

"But what about the prostitution? You get so upset when I go on a job."

"I'll get used to it, I guess."

"What about sex with other people?"

"I assume that's based on insecurity. I'm hoping that the more confident I am about our relationship, the less I'll feel threatened by any-body else." My mood changed. "Anyway, I don't have much choice."

"You do."

"What, go out with somebody else?"

"No, Rufus."

"What are you saying?"

"I'm saying okay."

I had to check to make sure I'd heard him right. "You wouldn't mind being monogamous?"

"If it's what you want, that's fine with me."

"Really?"

"Sure, Aswell."

"Somuch," I said in my best inbred-hillbilly twang, "yaw soo gurd ter mey." Then, serious: "How come you're so sure?"

"I love you. That's what I'm going with."

We stopped near a blossom-laden cherry tree. I told Luke to lie beneath it. He did so without question. Reaching up, I shook the tree vigorously. Petals floated down, covering him.

"That's how I always picture you," I said.

"This is how I picture you, too."

"Covered with flower petals?"

"No, shaking your arms in the air like a madman!"

During his stay, Luke and I didn't have sex with anyone else. He didn't cruise other men, and was everything I wished for in a boyfriend. I felt safe in our relationship, and looked forward to visiting him in San Francisco. I even began thinking about getting an apartment there.

16

Luke left on Thursday. One week, two rehearsals, and numerous transatlantic phone calls to my boyfriend later, a stripped-down version of Whatever—three vocalists and a minidisk of backing tracks—set off for Paris and a gig in a gay club called Queen. Nina and Marc met me at the Eurostar terminal in Waterloo Station, Nina looking like a very proper but very sexy schoolmistress, Marc in a yellow tartan suit made by a friend to match his now bright yellow hair. We settled in for the long train ride ahead.

We were booked at Queen that night. We hadn't performed for a while, so we were excited as we prepared on the train. Nina painted holographic varnish on her nails, continuing up her fingers. I asked how she'd thought of such a funny idea and she reminded me that I'd done it for her earlier in the year, on a coach going to some other concert, which made me wonder why I bothered having experiences since

I invariably forgot them. Marc played with different combinations of
jewelry as I twisted his hair into tight knots close to his scalp. With
hours to kill, we played Consequences. On a piece of paper, each person
drew a body part, concealed it by folding the paper, then passed it on to
the next person. Nina and Marc had bizarre imaginations, which made
the game fun. Marc was also skilled with a pen; his section always
looked the most slick.

We were met in Paris by Ran, the unassuming, elegant, well-spoken man
who'd organized the event, and taken to our hotel. At around four o'clock,
we went to Queen for a sound check—and discovered we were billed as a
sex show. We were at once pissed off and amused. After the sound check, we
met the artists Pierre and Gilles for dinner. Although the food was too
French for my liking, we had a lovely time, and left the restaurant with several bottles of red wine.

Back at the hotel, to give Marc a break (and for a change), I asked
Pierre and Gilles to draw on my body—something anatomical. They
were very patient and took great care; by the time they'd finished, I
looked like I'd been peeled. I downed a couple of Valiums and a beta-
blocker to make sure I wouldn't be nervous. When we thought we looked
okay and were drunk enough (which amounted to the same thing), we
set off for the club.

It was soon time to go on. More fucked up than nervous, we began
our set to an audience of blank-looking Parisian queens and ended it to
one of baffled-looking Parisian queens. Hardly surprising—Whatever's
sound was odd, combining contemporary elements like trip-hop and
harsh industrial drum loops underscored with classical orchestration.
Over this backup we sang my lyrics, by turns sinister and disturbingly
sweet. Each track was different from the next, one punk, another soul, the
next rap; then we all might join in for a folk-sounding chorus. We did our
own recording and used musicians according to what sound we wanted.

Papers around the world described us varyingly as "postmodern art-house," "cynical pop," and "apocalyptic musical theater."

I can't say whether the Queen-crowd liked us or not. My guess is they didn't. We didn't give a fuck; *we'd* had fun. A write-up in a Parisian newspaper said our performance had gone over the heads of the audience. We thought "under their legs" was probably more accurate. We'd made it clear that Whatever had nothing to do with porn; we'd even sent ahead recordings of our work and press photos. Despite this, the club had advertised us as a sex act, sealing their own fate.

We had one full day to rest before boarding another train, on which we were joined by a troupe of fellow freaks from Ibiza who were also booked to do a show in Brussels. Marc and I knew one of them from the Mayfair brothel we'd worked at after college.

Our rooms were at the top of the Hilton on the "executive" floor, which had its own café, where we sat for hours eating Belgian chocolates, drinking coffee, and staring out the huge windows at the city below. Nina and I decided to use the hotel gym, which consisted of four Stairmasters facing windows, a rowing machine, and lots of bottled water. The view was stunning; pounding away on one Stairmaster, I turned from watching the Brussels sunset to look at Nina beside me, and caught her doing the same. We laughed. "Lucky bastards," I said. "Sorry, *fortunate*."

We washed, dressed, and headed downstairs to the hotel bar filled with middle-class families whose sons couldn't take their eyes off Nina. Ran called and told us to have dinner in the hotel (apparently we'd be hard-pressed to find a better restaurant in town). We ate a lot and drank a couple of bottles of wine. It was quite late by the time we were finished and cabbed over to Ran's flat, where he chopped some white powder and we all did a line, not bothering to ask what it was.

Then we set off for the club.

Part Two
Useless Man

17

DAVID'S ACCOUNT

I assumed it was going to be a boring day. It was Easter Sunday, a bank holiday, a long weekend. Aiden was in Brussels with Marc and Nina. Most everyone else I knew probably had gone out the night before. Time dragged by. I would have to invent something to do. I decided to take a long walk on the south side of the Thames, into the city district, to look at other areas where I might want to live.

The phone rang. I was not in the mood to talk to anyone, so I let the machine answer.

"Hello, David? It's Nina. I just wanted to see how you were. I'll try back later."

It was strange that one of Aiden's friends should call me. Perhaps she wanted to break new ground. I went on my walk, came back, had lunch, sat for a while, and then called Nina.

"David! How are you doing?"

"I'm fine. How are you?"

"Marc called already, didn't he?"

"No. Why? What's going on?"

"You don't know? Fuck!"

"What's wrong?" I began to feel uneasy.

"It's Aiden. He's had an accident."

Fear overcame me. I imagined a world without him, cold and empty.

"He's alive. I can't tell you much more. He's in intensive care." She paused. "Are you okay?"

I could barely speak. "What happened?"

A brief story was relayed. Nina tried to be reassuring. I wanted to speak to Aiden, but he was unconscious. It wasn't until half an hour later that I thought to call the hospital. I spoke to the orthopedic surgeon who had worked on Aiden. He was friendly and tried to put my mind at ease.

Aiden had been hit in the head and his brain was swollen. He couldn't move the left side of his body. I decided to wait until I'd seen him before phoning his mother.

The next morning, I booked a flight to Brussels.

"Aiden, look who's here," said Nina.

I didn't recognize Aiden as I walked into intensive care. He had a tube up his nose, bandages round his head, staples in his stomach, and an IV drip. Tubes led from him, one for piss, one for blood. Even so, it was a great relief to see him.

He was coming round from the anaesthetic. I knew from experience how uncomfortable this was. He was very thirsty, but because of the brain swelling was only allowed to suck water from little sterile tissues. His whole body shook. I was surprised that he was able to laugh.

He had to stop himself, because it was painful. I was given an apron and gloves to wear.

During subsequent visits, a pattern emerged. Aiden would put one hundred percent into entertaining me, although his brain was so badly bruised, he couldn't think properly. He constantly mixed reality and fiction; it was never really clear if he was being playful or if he truly didn't have a clue. It was hard to know how far to go along with him. After all, his version of reality was more fun than the small, windowless room where he spent twenty-four hours a day in intensive care.

"Who's in the swimming pool, in the other room?" he said.

"There is no swimming pool in the other room," I said. This registered, but not for long.

"Debbie Harry's in the pool."

I tried to make sense of this. Chlorine was used to keep the unit clean. Perhaps the smell triggered the swimming pool idea. Aiden loved how Debbie Harry looked in one of Blondie's videos in which she wore a red-and-white-striped swimsuit. Another time, he spoke of going riding and wearing jodhpurs. The nurses had put bandages on his legs to prevent them from swelling; I imagined this was where the idea came from. Sometimes he'd ask, "Am I talking nonsense again?" at least half aware of the things he said.

I thought the fantasies might be an escape mechanism. The whole left side of his body was paralyzed. He seemed overappreciative of food and liquid, probably the only nice sensations available to him. He was very emotional. He cried at the thought of people coming all the way to Belgium to visit him.

He'd always been fond of wordplay, but his sharpness had increased. There were times when I was concerned about him getting tired, but the doctors seemed to think the stimulation was good for him. They expressed concern that his paralysis was not getting better, and ordered a brain scan. I imagined Aiden in a wheelchair for the rest of his life. I started to cry. Nina put her arm around me, stroked my head. We had never been so physical before.

"I cannot think of anything worse than paralysis," I said.

"Whatever happens," she said, taking hold of my hand, "it will be okay."

Despite the horrible possibilities, I felt that she was right. Nina and I became closer that day.

On Tuesday, taking the first flight he could get, Aiden's friend Joseph Holtzman arrived from New York. He was followed a day later by Flora, who flew in from London. On Thursday, Aiden's mother arrived with his brother Des. When they walked into the ward, Aiden cried. His mother seemed intent on getting a priest to visit. When asked what I thought, I said it might scare Aiden. Like all mums, she went ahead and did what she wanted, anyway. I think Aiden found it funny. I am sure he didn't approve. But he did it to make his mother happy. Even in the state he was in, he thought of her feelings rather than his own.

18

MARC'S ACCOUNT

After dinner we went to Ran's, then headed toward the club where we'd perform the following evening. In Brussels, the law only allows three passengers in a cab at a time; we split into twos, so that nobody traveled alone. Nina and Aiden went first, while Ran and I waited for another taxi to appear.

We drove out of town, into a forested area, along a dark road overhung with trees forming a long, winding tunnel. Finding no sign of the party, we turned around and drove for about a minute, then slowed down. The taxi's headlights picked up something, somebody lying in the road, leg bent at an odd angle.

It was Aiden.

I opened the door while the cab was still moving. As soon as it stopped, I lunged out.

"Aiden. Aiden!"

No response. He was unconscious. Something stirred in the darkness of my peripheral vision.

"Marc!" Nina was at my side.

"What happened?"

"We were hit by a car."

"Aiden. Baby, Aidy."

A stranger told me that he'd called an ambulance on his cell phone. I was relieved.

Aiden made a rasping sound.

"He's stopped breathing," said Nina. She lay at his side, cupping his head in her hands and breathing air into his lungs.

The forest was so quiet. I took off my denim jacket and laid it over Aiden, to shield him from the cold breeze. I located his pulse. It was fading. I had to remind Aiden to live.

"Your heart is getting weaker, baby," I urged, trying to encourage him. "Come on." It came across as panic.

"No. No!" Nina shouted.

I said something else to Aiden about his heart, probably stupid. The message felt crucial.

"Call an ambulance!" Nina screamed at distant silhouettes.

Time staggered by: freaky, slow. Somebody mentioned they had a car and that it might be quicker for them to take Aiden to the hospital. I pictured lifting him, broken, blood pouring from his body, into the back of a small car. Apparently, I was speaking my thoughts aloud. Nina agreed with me, and asked me to see what had been done about getting an ambulance. "But really ask them," she said. I imagined she meant I should scream, which I did: "Please! Call an ambulance!"

"I have called two times already," a voice with a French accent came from the darkness, sounding so sweet. "They say it's on its way."

Aiden's pulse got weaker. "Not Aiden, please. Not Aiden," I begged, a mixture of moaning and pure emotion.

Nina kept breathing into Aiden's lungs. Her fingers slipped into a hole on the side of his head. His ear was hanging off; blood pooled, dark, beneath his head. "No, no," I kept moaning.

Nina told Ran to take me away. I walked about six feet with him, briefly letting go of Aiden's hand, then squirmed from Ran's embrace and knelt beside Aiden again, saying, "I'm okay." The forest was quiet, except for the sound of the wind. I put my hands on Aiden's chest. "We love you, Aidy," I said. "The ambulance will be here soon." I sounded pathetic. I had no idea if it would be there soon or not.

Headlights closed in quickly from the distance: a police car, followed by an ambulance. We made room for the paramedics as the police asked us what had happened. I answered as best I could without taking my eyes off Aiden and the crowd that had gathered around him. An oxygen mask was put over his mouth. I shuddered as the elastic slipped into the wound between his severed ear and his head.

Three handsome women who had been at the party we'd been looking for offered to drive Nina and me to the hospital, where they were doctors. As I helped Nina into their car, she turned to me and said softly, "We were lying in the road."

At the hospital, we smoked cigarettes and waited, and I prayed; it seemed the only thing to do. Aiden was in the best place for his body, but the Aiden inside that body needed all the help he could get.

Nina also needed medical attention, and was eventually seen by a doctor. I couldn't help noticing how beautiful he was. He had a rugged, outdoors look. His hair was very blond, probably bleached on a recent sunny holiday. His skin was perfect. I hoped this man would be the first thing Aiden saw when he opened his eyes.

The things I remember next were fragmented. Lemon-flavored Perrier.

Magazines covering a table. A headline that read "CRASH," which barely distracted me. Cigar smoke. A scary, intriguing man who'd been in a fight tried to start a conversation. I was grateful. I couldn't speak French, but enjoyed watching his face form words. I think he was trying to tell me what had happened to him.

Nina lay across some chairs. The doctor who came with news of Aiden knelt on one knee beside her head, speaking in French, his voice grave. When I asked Nina to interpret, the doctor said, "Oh, sorry," and repeated himself in perfect English. Aiden was alive, breathing with backup. We were told to go home, get some rest, and return later.

It was dawn.

Nina's room at the hotel was on the way to mine. About ten feet from her door, she collapsed, making a noise like an animal in pain. I managed to get her into the room. Then we both lost control, sliding against the wall to the floor, crying and holding each other desperately, half-comforting, half-grasping. Eventually, Nina staggered into bed.

It seemed I should stay awake—some kind of vigil or prayer. Be strong, I repeated in my head. I went to my room, had a bath, and thought of Aiden, how much I loved him. It was now Easter Sunday, I realized, and thought of Nina and Mary Magdalene. I shaved and got dressed, trying to normalize myself, then sat in the twenty-fourth-floor café watching a drizzly, gray Brussels. A few hours later, unable to wait any longer, I roused Nina from her tablet-induced slumber.

A nurse took us down a long, dimly lit corridor where a doctor joined us and escorted us to Aiden's room in intensive care. He was tied to a bed, his head covered in white bandages. He'd lost the use of the left side of his body. He looked at us. Nina showered him in kisses.

"Where are we?" he said, his speech slurred.

"In Brussels," said Nina. "We were hit by a car."

"Oh, yeah. We made a mistake, didn't we?"

"Yes, but it's okay. It's okay, baby."

Out of nowhere, he said, "I feel like I've just split up with somebody."

"*We* love you," I said.

Nina and I leaned over Aiden, cooing and soothing, stroking him. Suddenly I felt hot, my head heavy. I began to sweat. I was going to faint.

Nina had Aiden's attention, so I made my way down the bed toward the door. It was ajar. I took hold of the handle and went from standing to kneeling. I leaned over. My face made contact with the cool floor. Somebody told me to stay down a minute. A nurse offered me water. Be strong, I thought. Aiden needs you. Breathe. Get over it, you silly thing.

The nurse helped me up. "A lot of people react this way to intensive care," she said.

"I'm okay," I said.

I went back into the room, to the bed . . . and started to faint again.

19

NINA'S ACCOUNT

We were having a fun evening. The weather was warm, we were happy to be together; there was a special, almost romantic feel to it. We decided to see the club where we'd be doing our gig the next day. Aiden and I got there first and had to wait for Ran and Marc. I went to have a pee, lifting my skirt and squatting beside the road, which led into woods. Aiden ran toward me, laughing and peeing. I scurried into the woods, laughing myself, still peeing. It wasn't the first time Aiden had tried to pee on me. When we were happy, we often regressed like this.

Aiden walked out of the woods ahead of me. I turned to examine the shadows of the trees. "Nina, look at the stars," I heard Aiden calling.

He was lying in the road, staring into the sky. I joined him. After a few moments, I became aware of distant lights approaching us. I got to my feet and pulled Aiden by his hand, trying to force him to rise. "Aiden, get up, there's a car coming!" He didn't respond.

Glaring lights. Impact. I was in the air, spinning head over heels.

The next thing I remember is crouching in the road. Somehow, I'd landed on my feet—thanks no doubt to instincts developed from years of training as a gymnast. Aiden lay some distance from me. I scrambled over to him, one of my legs giving way.

His eyes were closed. A pool of blood was spreading behind his head. His breathing was labored; his chest rattled. I began to blow air into his open mouth, firmly and consistently, trying to breathe life into him. I felt no separation between us; at that moment, his life was my life. I was calm. I cupped my hand gently around his head and his blood poured into it.

The other taxi must have arrived, because Marc was there. And people around us. Someone pointed out that Aiden's leg looked funny. Marc began screaming. I asked him to stop. Calm was essential. I was brusque and bossy. I kept breathing into Aiden's lungs. Marc left, walked around in circles, came back, took Aiden's pulse. It was getting weaker. He told Aiden to breathe, not to give up living. I stopped what I was doing, to see if Aiden could breathe without me. He couldn't. I resumed blowing deeply into him.

I've no idea how long it was until the ambulance finally arrived and the medics took over. As I left them to their efforts, I noticed two cars in the road, one with a broken windscreen. There must have been a car crash, I thought. (Later, Ran told me that the glass had been shattered by the impact with my body. I don't recall this at all.) I was taken, limping, to the side of a police van and repeatedly asked simple questions. A woman put her arm around me. Someone brought me one of my shoes, which had been flung to the other side of the road. The high heel had broken off. I barely saw what was being done now to my friend, who had a cluster of uniformed backs around him. Radios crackled as I sat shaking beside the van.

Aiden was strapped into a stretcher and put into the ambulance. I wanted to go with him, but wasn't allowed. The woman comforting me said she'd take me to the hospital. I have a slight recollection of small talk in the car. At the hospital, someone took me to a room and laid me down. Once alone, I limped back to the waiting room, to Marc. The same helpful woman put a blanket around me. I was still shaking. A nurse told me I should wash the blood off my hands. "No, I won't!" I responded hysterically. "If this is the last of Aiden I have, I want to keep him!"

My right leg was now very swollen. I was wearing only one shoe, without a heel. One of my flesh-tone stay-up stockings hung around my ankle. I kept limping backward and forward. I was told he was alive but unconscious, and advised to go home. I spent the night in a nightmare of not knowing if Aiden would regain consciousness.

The next day, the staff at the hospital told us he'd been hit on the head and had a damaged ear and a broken femur. He was still not stable enough for an operation. When Aiden regained consciousness, he could hardly speak. His head was bandaged and he had tubes coming in and out of him. Still, he looked beautiful.

I wish I could remember the order of events more precisely, but my memory is blurred. All I know is there were stages. First: Is he alive? Second: Will he come out of his coma? Then: Will he be *compos mentis*? The doctors performed daily checks and answered questions as quickly as they could. As part of a mental health check, Aiden was asked, "Where are you?" With throwaway charm, he said, "Brussels, apparently." This made everyone laugh. He still had his sense of humor. It was such a relief. When we told him his mother was coming to see him, he said, "You *are* joking." Then, after a pause, "This must be serious."

His mouth drooped to the left. His left eye didn't open or close, but rested sleepily between the two states. He couldn't move his left leg, his left arm, or any of the fingers of his left hand. Nevertheless, Aiden became well enough to be operated on. The surgeon, who was clearly affected by his charismatic patient, sewed Aiden's ear back into place, repaired his damaged liver, and put a metal pin through his femur.

I visited once a day. The process of getting there was painful and exhausting. Aiden had an evolving support network. He started to be able to move his left hand slightly. One of the doctors said this was a good sign and we could look forward to full recovery of movement. I was happy, as I'd been facing the possibility of Aiden never walking again. After a brain scan, another doctor told us we shouldn't expect miracles, dumping me back into fear.

Aiden became preoccupied with fluids. As I arrived each day, he'd demand I fetch him a vodka cranberry from the bar. He was very thirsty, and not allowed to drink. He hated being tied to the bed (to prevent the drips being pulled out), and would try to get up to go to the toilet. He was often confused and forgot who'd visited.

Aiden's mother left secretly one day. She didn't want to say good-bye, in case it upset him, and she didn't want to see him cry anymore. I think, maybe, *she* didn't want to cry anymore, either. Everybody thought it best not to tell Aiden she had gone. This worked well. He didn't mention it, so we assumed he hadn't noticed.

After a week, he was moved from intensive care and his real discomfort began. The nurses were rough, he said, and he was in pain. He begged me for painkillers. He wanted to go back to London, to the Chelsea and Westminster Hospital, which was only a short distance from his flat. I didn't have much hope that this could happen. He needed supervision, and he wouldn't be able to sit in a normal airplane seat.

David managed to organize a flight home, through an insurance company. It cost two thousand pounds. Strapped into a stretcher, Aiden was brought on board before the other passengers, then laid across a row of three seats. By the end of the flight, Aiden needed to pee. The supervising nurses told him he would have to go in a bottle. He tried, of course, but couldn't pee. He was in public, with only a blanket to cover him; it must have been so degrading. He was so traumatized that even in the ambulance driving into London, he couldn't go. He had to be fitted with a catheter at the hospital before he could finally relieve himself. I bless nature's gift of Aiden's amnesia.

20

A hospital. I'm the patient. I've been injured, badly. There are bandages all over me. I'm in a bed, in the corner of a ward. A curtain made from a weird orange fabric opens and closes. People move in front of me. Some I know; they're emotional, chipper, or crying. Others, I don't know: patients, nurses, doctors. In the bed opposite mine, a Spanish girl watches TV all day and seems to argue with most of her visitors. I hear some of what she says, and even understand a little of it. The gay man in the bed next to me doesn't have any visitors and rarely speaks, but I hear clearly the noises his body makes. The body in my bed seems unfamiliar, with a rubber tube leading out the end of its dick to a bag of piss. I'm wearing what looks like a nappy. It's all a mystery.

Being so heavily medicated, I didn't know to care. Day by day, things began to make more sense. I realized I was at Chelsea and Westminster, near my home in London. Marc and David visited daily. Nina didn't.

Apparently, her leg hurt badly and she was having trouble getting around. Marc told me this. A couple of other friends visited, I think. I remember Josie Jones and her girlfriend, Annie, a professional chef, bringing delicious multicourse gourmet meals. I'm hoping I've forgotten who visited, rather than that people didn't bother to come. My mum, my dad, and Des came. I assume the whole family did, but again, I don't remember.

Some of the nurses gave me hope, just by being kind, standing at my bedside with beaming smiles and managing to express love even doing trivial chores. Other nurses were cold. My mum had masses said for me in her local church—and all over the world, via relatives and friends. This didn't comfort me, although it made me love her even more.

Marc and David took turns visiting, so that I always had company. David spent whole days beside my bed. Last thing at night, he brushed my teeth, using a beaker as a makeshift basin, into which I'd spit. I still couldn't make it to the bathroom; the water supply was bottled. David generally waited until I fell asleep, holding my hand in his on the pillow, against my face. This was a huge comfort, as I was often frightened. I'm sure that in a different way he was, too. Surely David was what I'd always wanted, always looked for, when reaching out to another man, but it took this situation for me to be able to ask for it. Naturally, David gave. Something was happening between us. Maybe it was love, or maybe just my perception due to the morphine I was taking, but I became a vessel, desperate for this love. David simply poured.

Marc's approach was different. He pressed me to do things—get out of bed, have a shower, go somewhere in my wheelchair—anything other than stare at the orange curtain around my bed. I didn't feel like doing anything, and had become attached to the privacy and security the curtain afforded. The fact that I hadn't had a real bath in over a month didn't faze me. I intentionally hadn't left my bed since being transferred from

Belgium (although I had fallen out twice). In an attempt to shut Marc up, however, I finally agreed to have a shower.

Getting into the wheelchair was a new experience. In Chelsea and Westminster one can travel round each floor and see down the atrium to the people below. I asked Marc to take me on a tour. As he wheeled me through the corridors, I became aware that I was disabled. Men and women seemed to look away from me. Children stared. Soon, I'd had enough.

"My shower, please," I said to Marc.

"Would sir be needing some ruffian to scrub his back?"

"I don't think that will be necessary."

"Why, can you reach?"

"No, but I don't care if my back's dirty."

Ordinarily, the shower would have made me cringe, with its disgusting lime scale–coated plastic seat and supports to lean on folding down from the wall, but I'd decided to go through with it. Marc checked the water temperature, helped me off with my socks, and covered my head with a plastic bag to protect the bandage. Before leaving the wheelchair, I opened my bathrobe and freed my hands and arms. In an awkward motion, I stood up, leaving the robe on the wheelchair. Supporting most of my weight on the hand rails, I carefully moved forward into the shower, turned, and lowered myself onto the seat. My leg, which I had to keep straight, stuck out of the stall. The water flowed over me.

"See," said Marc, "that's not so bad, hey?"

I lifted my head to him, water streaming down my face. "It feels beautiful," I said. "Thank you. It was a good idea." Water entered my mouth as I talked; I lowered my head to stop it.

For the first time since my accident, I saw my naked body. Saw the dressing on my hip where the surgeon had entered to insert the metal bar into the bone, the bunches of stitches all over my stomach, a huge scab next to my knee where the original traction had been.

I started to cry.

"Baby!" said Marc and, fully clothed, got into the shower with me. "Whatever, forever," he comforted, sitting down and putting his arms around me.

I tried to copy what he'd said. "Whatever . . ." It was no good. I was crying too much to form proper words, full of fear, confusion, disappointment, and self-pity.

"I mean *forever*," he said, squeezing me firmly.

Marc managed to get me dried and back into bed. I was expecting a visit from Des and Lucy. By the time they arrived, I was sitting, drinking a cup of vending-machine hot chocolate.

I received quite a lot of cards in hospital. Some seemed phony, with clichéd sentiments, and went straight into the trash. More than ever, honesty was important to me. Lee Freeman, the promoter who ran DTPM ("Delirium Tremors Post Meridien," the hugely popular ongoing Sunday night event), sent me flowers and a note saying "We miss you down at the club." Alexander McQueen, the fashion designer, sent flowers and a note saying "Rest your lallies, love." None of my other always-so-pleased-to-see-you-kiss-and-let's-do-a-line club friends even sent a word-of-mouth "get well"—despite the fact that I'd been going to clubs since I was fourteen. Some people are better at this kind of thing than others, I knew, but it registered deeply who bothered to show they gave a damn, and I couldn't help feeling resentful of those who didn't.

Immediately after the accident, I wasn't cognizant enough to call Luke, but David, Marc, or Nina must have let him know what had happened because eventually he called to apologize for not coming to see me. He had no way of assessing how badly injured I was; my brain was so scrambled, I spoke nonsense. Nevertheless, it's surprising how soon I noticed and how bothered I was that Luke didn't visit me. Of course, he simply might not have been able to afford the trip to London, or to take time away from work. Whatever the reason, the reality was that within a relatively short time we stopped speaking on the phone. I continued to feel affection for Luke, but little respect. Besides, I'd experienced something greater. I'd held David's hand.

21

The entire left side of my body was still paralyzed, and in areas there was no sensation on my skin. A brain scan revealed that nerves had been severed. One doctor told me that, in time, the damage might—or might not—repair itself. I dreaded the idea of being in hospital long-term, and pleaded to be allowed to go home. On condition that I had someone to take care of me twenty-four hours a day, my wish was granted. David offered to move in with me.

Whereas life in hospital revolved around my bed, once home it consisted mainly of me lying on the sofa, with David looking after me. My world became tiny: two-and-a-half feet by five feet, to be exact. Everything I needed—address book, HIV meds, TV remote controls—was close at hand, tucked between and under the cushions. The opposite wall was the thing I saw most, interrupted only by television, bath, bed, David, Marc, and the occasional less-close friend. To pass the time, I took

Valium, sleeping tablets, and hash, rotating them to avoid building up tolerance. Some days, I took too much, and when friends like Flora and Baillie came by, I hardly registered their visit, even though both were very dear to me and I was the godfather of Flora's baby, Louis. I was in some kind of semisleep mode, maybe even shut down. Everything felt chaotic. I hadn't finished cleaning, repairing, and organizing my flat since renting it out, and now I wasn't able to. With David's stuff added, it was cluttered. If I wanted to go from one room to the next, there had to be a really good reason; otherwise, rather than my getting into the wheelchair, David went for me. He did nearly everything for me: cooked my meals, emptied the urine container I'd now progressed to, and, when I went to bed, tucked me in and gave me a good-night kiss. I'd wake up periodically in darkness and lie as still as possible, for fear of something hurting, and always in the center of the bed, because it felt more secure and minimized the likelihood of my falling out.

Everything was new and different, but not in a way that made it interesting or exciting. I tried to create order, the first step, I imagined, toward having a life I liked. I got up, went to bed, and ate at set times. I watched weekly sitcoms in sequence, something I'd never before been able to manage.

In time, I was able to get into my wheelchair on my own, which meant I had more independence. This evolved into being able to move around on crutches, which opened up a whole other realm of possibilities. At first it felt weird, but I got used to it. Dinosaur-like, I went about my daily routine. It was only a fraction of what I used to be able to do, but I felt a certain achievement. David would have helped me if asked, but I wanted to feel I was making progress. My confidence grew. One morning I decided to attempt taking a bath.

Organizing all my body parts was complicated. The transition from wheelchair to bath felt part athletics, part mathematics, and part luck.

Once in, I did my version of physiotherapy, trying to bend my foot underneath me to stretch my knee joint (it didn't go anywhere much), after which I'd try to touch my hands to my toes (a bit easier). A greater challenge involved getting out of the bath. It was strenuous, yet comical, and it took a lot of concentration. Psyching myself up, I'd say aloud, "Come on, Aiden," reach for the towel hanging on the radiator behind me, and put it on the floor beside the tub. Next, I'd pull the plug—I'd heard that people could drown in mere inches of water—and wait until the bath emptied completely. To actually get out, I had to extend my hands and arms over the sides of the tub, as though I were diving, then hitch my good leg over the side, hovering on the edge for only a moment before sliding all the way until my knee reached the floor (being careful not to trap or squash my balls in the process). With my good arm and leg I then dragged the rest of me after, until I was kneeling on all fours. From there it was relatively easy. I dried some of my body in this position, then bundled myself awkwardly back into the wheelchair—relieved, exhausted, and a little surprised that it had all gone according to plan— before drying the rest of myself as best I could and wheeling myself out of the bathroom.

I don't know how effective these efforts were, but at least I felt like I was doing something to get better. And it took a long time. But time was something I had a lot of, and bathing soon became the focus of my day. Once, my wheelchair got stuck in the living room doorway when the phone rang. "Don't worry, I'll get it!" I shouted to David, and struggled to get there before the answering machine picked up. Using the sofa to balance, I pulled myself erect, tilted, and kind of lay forward over the armrest, reaching for the receiver. I managed to grab it, but in doing so fell on my face, backside in the air.

"Hello?" I said.

"Hello. Have I caught you at a bad time?"

"Not particularly," I lied, feeling completely ridiculous.

"Good. You don't know me. I'm calling in answer to an ad."

"That must be years old."

"Do you still do this work?"

"No."

"Are you opposed to it?"

"I guess not."

"Good. I've seen your videos. I'm very interested."

I should have hung up, but the man seemed fairly pleasant and I didn't want to be rude.

"You've got a fine physique."

I felt uneasy. "Not really," I said.

"You're being modest."

"No." How could I even begin to explain my situation without crying?

"Is it not convenient for you to see me?" said the man, now feeding me my lines.

"That's right," I said.

"I'm sorry."

"It's no problem."

"Maybe another time?"

"Sure."

We said good-bye.

I didn't know why I'd agreed with him. I couldn't imagine being naked in front of somebody ever again, let alone being paid for it.

It was a gloomy day. The lights needed turning on. I sighed and arranged my legs in front of me on the sofa, and unintentionally stared down at them. My thoughts were blurred, but clearly unhappy. David came into the living room.

"Good boy," he said. "Who was it?"

"A punter," I said incredulously.

"What time is he booked for?"

"The year 3000."

David laughed. I didn't. He crouched beside the wheelchair. "You can't see a punter," he said. "Your hair's a mess."

"Then it matches the rest of me."

"That's not true."

My eyes began to water. "Why is this taking so long?" I said.

"Baby!"

"I'm so bored of being cooped up, not being able to do anything."

"So let's get out of the house, do something."

"What could we do?" I said. "Anywhere we go has to have wheelchair access."

"That can't be too difficult these days."

"Virgin Cinemas have just been refurbished. They must have taken wheelchairs into account."

David called to find out. Virgin Chelsea had no wheelchair access and lots of steps—no go. We opted for Virgin Fulham Road, where two of the screens had only a few steps. We decided to leave my "wheels" at home and "go on crutch."

Seeing as how we were going to the trouble to get me out of the apartment, we decided to make a day of it and do some shopping, too. Sainsbury's, a short, relatively scenic drive away. We parked in the disabled area, because it was closer to the toilet. (Pissing had become something of a psychological issue since leaving the hospital and having my catheter removed. I had to piss more often; if for some reason I couldn't, I got a very uncomfortable, burning sensation. So I liked to know that a toilet was nearby.)

David ran inside the store while I waited in the car. It was nice to have a few minutes to myself. I needed help so consistently, I rarely had time alone. My window was lowered slightly, enough for a cool summer breeze to drift inside. I tilted back my head, closed my eyes, and felt a kind of happiness, at least somewhat at peace.

Loud tapping startled me. I opened my eyes on an elderly woman, heavily made up, with sculpted hair. Using the back of her hand, she struck her rings aggressively against the driver's-side window, making the most noise possible, shouting, "You! You!"

I leaned over and let down the window. "Hello," I said.

"What are you doing parked here?"

"I'm waiting for a friend."

"You're not disabled. You shouldn't be parked here."

"I can't walk. Is that disabled enough?"

"Rubbish!"

I was shocked. All I could think to say was, "Why are you being so horrible?"

"Where's your wheelchair?" she demanded.

"I left it at home," I answered. Realizing this might sound like I was joking, I turned as much as I could and said, "I'll be using those," gesturing at my crutches.

"Rubbish!" she said again. "You're not disabled."

"We'll only be a few minutes."

"You shouldn't be taking up disabled spaces."

Any other time I would have agreed, but there were plenty of empty disabled parking spots. "Surely these spaces are to make life easier for people having difficulty," I said, trying to be reasonable.

"Yes. That's not you. Where's your badge?" She was referring to an orange badge the London Council issued to the disabled, which was supposed to be on view at all times.

"I've only been out of hospital a short while." I hoped this would appeal to a more generous part of her nature.

"So why haven't you got a badge?"

The woman was possessed. She continued to rant. I leaned over and pressed the button. The window went up. Her head was so far into the car, she had to jerk away to avoid being choked. "You cheeky bastard," she sputtered.

At first, her language surprised me, then I realized it suited her. I reclined my head and closed my eyes again. Unfortunately, I could still hear her muffled voice.

"I'm going to get a security guard," she threatened, more irate than ever.

"Good," I said. I couldn't believe anyone else would be as insensitive. She left. The car was silent.

More tapping: David. He pulled an ugly face. He looked so beautiful.

We dropped off the groceries at home, with just enough time to get to the cinema. We picked up our tickets, got popcorn, and made our way to our screen. It was dark and there were five steps, which scared me, so David went ahead of me in case I fell. I managed the steps without too much difficulty, but found sitting down more challenging, not knowing when to let my weight off the crutches. I think it was the darkness, but also my lack of balance. All went relatively smoothly until I needed to pee, about halfway through the film. I'd been both dreading and expecting this. David had already agreed to accompany me. I stood up, holding the seat in front for balance.

We slowly made our way to the bathroom for disabled people. It was nearer than the regular ones, which I appreciated. Getting there, my mood changed instantly. It was locked. David went to look for someone with a key. He returned with a young man.

"Why is the door locked?" I said. "Surely it defeats the purpose."

"If it's not locked, everyone uses it."

"Yes, but how am I meant to find you?"

"I'm sorry, but it's the policy. I could give you a refund."

"If I wanted the money instead of seeing the film I would have stayed at home."

"I'm sorry, sir."

"No, *I'm* sorry. I know it's not your fault, but please mention it to someone in charge."

"I'll do that," he said. "I'm sorry again."

"Cheers. *I'm* sorry, again."

Despite the fact that I'd taken plenty of strong painkillers, I was uncomfortable sitting through the rest of the film. It was nice to get out of the house, though. I felt almost normal.

22

Gradually, my paralysis improved and I could do things I previously hadn't been able to. I didn't feel horny, but I was interested to see what, if anything, would happen if I jerked off.

I lay in bed, stretching my arms to make sure I was in the center, then squeezed my dick. There wasn't much sensation, but I persevered until eventually it got plumper. I tried thinking of sexy things, but nothing kept my interest for long. I pictured Luke, hoping he could at least be relied on for this. Apparently not; I could kid myself only so much. My mind was more concerned with medical issues: pain, paralysis, lack of sensation. I tried again, focusing on a porn actor I'd worked with. We were having real sex. I began to feel something I recognized. Images flashed through my mind, nostalgic and exciting. Sensation seemed to build; I edged into it. With a lot more effort, I came. But it felt different from how I remembered, subtler, less black-and-white.

Instead of subsiding instantly, my orgasm continued, pulsating, easing off slowly. Perhaps this was because the left side of my groin was still partially paralyzed, or because masturbating was foreign to me now. In any case, it felt great.

I went to sleep, but each time my pills wore off, pain would wake me. After a night of tossing fitfully from one aching body part to another, I woke resentful and directed my irritation at Luke. *He said he loved me*, I thought, *but clearly he didn't.* This shouldn't have surprised me. It was completely reasonable that somebody should change his mind or simply not follow through. The only problem was that I was desperate enough in my life now to care.

The sounds of David getting up in the next room distracted me, allowing my mood to change. Listening to David potter around the flat reassured me. I lifted my duvet and organized my body into a sitting position on the side of my bed. With a great deal of effort I stood, using my crutches as both a support and climbing frame. As usual, I waited a few seconds before attempting to walk, to make sure I wasn't dizzy.

"Hado!" I shouted. This was my way of saying, "Hello, good morning, I love you," to David.

"Hado," he replied. I think he meant the same.

I wobbled forward on my crutches, popping my head into David's room and saying, "Any chance of coffee?" I moved on to the toilet where, balancing precariously, I peed, then undressed as I ran a bath. In the hall outside the bathroom was a full-length mirror. Naked, I turned to face it. I couldn't help focusing on the scar at my hip. After that, all I could see were bony shoulders and atrophied leg muscles. I forced myself to stop dwelling on these, only to discover an inch-thick deposit of fat on my tummy.

I reminded myself that when I'd needed it most, my body had pulled through—with Nina's help—and now it was repairing itself, that the slightest change in circumstance—inches or seconds this way or that, the weather or the driver's mood—could have left me permanently paralyzed or limbless. Or dead. (Even my foggy mind was getting clearer.) I'd always viewed my life as pedestrian, but now I longed for even a part of that commonplace existence. And for the body I used to have.

I leaned against the bathroom sink and looked closely at my face. My expression was softer. My eyes looked wary, resigned, but somehow exhilarated. *I know you*, I thought. *And . . . I like you.* I smiled. I sat on the edge of the tub and sighed deeply. In the water, I soaked, stared, and sank into myself. I gently stretched my left leg, pulling my knee toward my chin. As though suddenly realizing something—how lucky I'd been?—I pulled my knee to my face and kissed it.

David came into the bathroom. "Coffee break," he said.

"*Break* from what?"

"From being unhappy."

"Great."

"How do you feel?"

"Flabby, skinny, self-indulgent."

"Same as usual!"

"Yeah, only not as pretty."

"Do you fancy going for a drive?"

"Yeah!" I said, excited. "Hang on, though, it's a holiday weekend. The roads will be really busy."

"Let's try anyway."

In the bedroom, I lay down to put on my boxers and jeans, so I could wiggle into them. I had developed special ways of doing everything. But though I tried to work out the most efficient methods, as a rule the simplest tasks were arduous and draining. With my socks and trainers, it felt like pure contortion. If I got an arm caught in a sleeve or couldn't manage buttons, I'd call out and David would come to my rescue. Today, for the first time, I managed it by myself, due in part to my choice of outfit: a sweatshirt and baggy shorts.

David prepared cereal and another cup of coffee. I brushed my teeth in my wheelchair; it was easier than trying to balance. I'd learned the basics with my crutches quite well, but if I was holding myself up, I never had a free hand. I could get from one place to another, but was unable to do much once I got there. I'm sure in time people find ways around this, but I couldn't work it out at all.

Finally, David and I made our way to the car. The summer air was loaded with fragrance. It was gorgeous, but I was miserable. Thoughts of Luke circulated in my brain—hardly surprising since I had so much time to think and was in no fit state to meet anybody else. I should have taken up a hobby, anything to occupy myself, but it was easier to moan and berate myself for my relationship not working. (I say *my* relationship because it had little to do with Luke. It was more about loneliness, aging, childhood fantasies of marriage, probably even something to do with being gay and wanting to be normal.)

The roads were busy; we decided to turn back. By the time we got home, I was worn out. I flopped onto the sofa. A few minutes later, David brought me a sandwich and a glass of skimmed milk. He sat on his sofa, opposite mine.

"Are you all right?" he said.

"I feel horrible."

"Why?"

"I don't know. Things seem to be getting to me. I . . ."

I started crying.

David came and sat beside me. "Baby," he said. "Everything's going to be okay."

By now I was sobbing. "I can't do the simplest things."

"You manage really well."

"It seems like I kill time all day watching the clock, waiting for this to be over."

David put his arms around me. "You've got so much better," he said.

"I want my life to be like it was."

"You're getting there, baby."

"But no Luke now."

"Maybe that's a good thing."

"What do you mean?"

"It seems to me he's been insincere. When you needed him, he wasn't there. He can't even be bothered to call."

No matter how well I deluded myself, David only let me go so far before he'd help me see more clearly.

"He said he loved me."

"Do you think that was true?"

I paused. "I don't know."

"Do you really care?"

I laughed. Then, uncertainty in my voice, I said, "No?" My expression must have given away more than I intended.

"You called him, didn't you."

This wasn't really a question, and I didn't answer.

That night when David tucked me into bed, he said, "Are you okay?"

"Yeah, why do you ask?"

"Because Luke didn't call back."

"I didn't expect him to," I said.

I think David was beginning to be bugged by Luke. Or rather, that my fantasy and the reality were so different, and I was having such trouble seeing this.

"It's not that much to ask," said David. "Is it?"

I fell asleep confused and upset. In the morning I still felt upset, but a little less confused. Later that day, when David was out, I called Luke again. I got his machine, and pressed the hash button to bypass his pornstar–sounding message.

"Luke, it's Aiden. Just wanted to let you know I'm thinking of coming to Frisco."

Within minutes, Luke called back.

"Were you out?" I said.

"Kind of. The toilet." He sounded annoyed.

"So, what do you think of me coming over?"

Silence. Then, "This month's bad for me. My brother-in-law's coming for the first two weeks. I'm working out of town during the last two."

"What about the following month?" I needed that much time to get fit and strong enough to travel.

"The last week is free."

"You mean, I won't be charged?"

"We've got a special rate for Brits that month."

"What does it include?"

Before he could answer, my doorbell rang. I knew it would take me a while to answer it, and told Luke I'd ring him back. Leaning against the wall, I pressed the intercom button.

"Hello, beautiful," said a voice I instantly recognized.

"Ronalto!"

I buzzed him in and opened the door to a face all smiles and cheekiness. After a clumsy hug, he followed me into the living room and sat next to me on the sofa. Ronalto and I'd had sex every few months since we'd met. Whenever he visited, I'd give him a kiss, sometimes picking him up and carrying him straight into the bedroom. But that was before Luke and the accident.

Ronalto laughed. I waited. Ronalto was Brazilian, and his English was a little difficult to understand at times. This had the effect of making me listen more carefully. Receiving no answer, I said, "What?"

"I'm scared of hurting you," he said, shifting in his seat.

"How would you hurt me?"

"'Cause I want you, boy. You're so beautiful."

Carefully, he reached for me. A bit surprised, my first thoughts were of how I should respond. As much as I liked Ronalto, getting turned on wasn't something I could take for granted now. But I was keen to know what would happen, if I could still have sex. After a moment of holding him—his body odor, his seemingly pore-free skin, the heat rising off his body—I felt a twinge in my crotch. I waited to see if it endured. It did.

"Let's lie down," I said.

"Are you sure?"

"Yeah. I warn you, though, I'm a bit fragile."

"When was the last time you had sex?"

"Months ago."

"Wow!"

"Believe me, there's nothing *wow* about it."

"I'm glad you decided to do it with me."

"How could I resist?"

"I missed you."

In bed, Ronalto knelt over me as he'd always done, one knee either side my hips. This sent me into autopilot, where I acknowledged my bodily responses only after they occurred. He spat into his hand, rubbed it on my dick, sat down. With lots of wiggling and groaning, his ass enveloped my dick. It felt incredible. Although Ronalto didn't have HIV and knew I did, he always wanted my dick in his ass without a condom. Within seconds, he came. I took my dick out, jerked it, and did the same. Again, that prolonged spasm of climax.

Once calm and nuzzled into me, he said, "Were you worried about having sex?"

"Yeah."

"I tried my best not to hurt you, beautiful."

"Thank you," I said. Ronalto fell quiet. "What are you thinking?" I asked.

He paused before answering. "Before I go to bed at night, I pray."

"Put in a good word for me."

"I already have." Ronalto struggled with the words. "I asked Him to watch over you, to make you well."

I couldn't help focusing on his lips; they seemed like a child's. I squeezed him, wanting to kiss the lips that said those words. "I love you, boy," he whispered in my ear. "Be careful in future." I pressed my mouth against his shoulder. How smooth his skin was. He felt like a gift.

"Have you seen these scars?"

"How could they do that to my boy?" Generously, he spoiled me. "You may not feel sexy at the moment, but you are still very beautiful. You know that, don't you?" Only Ronalto could say the word *beautiful* over and over again without it seeming contrived.

"I appreciate you saying so."

"I mean it. You'll feel better when you get back to the gym, but you're lovely now. Believe me. I want to squeeze you?"

"You can. It's only my leg and ear you have to avoid."

He squeezed me lightly. I squeezed him harder.

"Are you hungry?" he said. "Let me cook for you."

There was no stopping him. He had a special dish in mind, and went to the store for ingredients—twice (when he returned the first time, he realized there was no salt and set off again). He must have run, because he was back within minutes. He served me on the sofa. After dinner, he left. His girlfriend was expecting him at home.

In my bedroom that night, balancing on my crutches, I looked at the picture Luke had given me for Christmas. For a moment, I fell into a reverie about being cuddled up with him. I thought to call him, then changed my mind. My relationship with whatever it was that Luke gave me had gone on long enough. I made my way into the kitchen and put the picture in the trash.

23

The café in Kew Gardens was noisy with insects, saturated with color, untidy with people. David and Marc and I took our sandwiches and tea and headed to an area that looked quieter. It was the height of summer, 1997. Children ran about. I stared at them.

"I want to try walking," I announced.

"Are you sure that's a good idea?" said David. "When did the doctor say you could?"

"I can't remember."

"Then maybe you should wait a bit longer," said Marc.

"That doesn't sound like the Marc I know and love."

"I'm just afraid the bone isn't mended yet," he said.

"Be afraid. Be very afraid. David, can I have your shoulder for support?"

"Of course."

I pulled myself up slowly and put my crutches behind me on my wheelchair, tentatively moving my left leg forward and resting my weight on my right. Easy enough. I shifted cautiously onto my left leg, carefully moved my right foot forward . . . and took a step.

"Oh, my God," said Marc.

"Good boy!" said David.

"Look at me."

"We see ya, child," said Marc. "Praise the Lord. It's a miracle."

Taking a few unsteady steps, I said, "Jesus Christ, it feels so unnatural!"

"Do you want your chair?" said Marc.

"No, I quite like this walking thing."

"I bet it catches on," said David.

"Do you think?"

"Soon everyone will be doing it," said Marc. "You watch."

"Burn that chair," I said, and stumbled. David caught me.

"Be careful, baby," said Marc.

"I'm not very good at careful."

"In that case, let me see you lap that rhododendron."

"That might be pushing it."

"You can do it," said David.

"Okay. Watch this."

My legs felt as though they were moving of their own accord and just happened to do what I wanted them to. I got halfway round the bush and caught sight of Marc on the other side.

"It's Superlegs," he said.

"They're not my best feature, but thanks all the same. Would you guys mind waiting here while I go for a short run?"

"You *are* kidding," said Marc.

"Yes!"

"It would surprise me, but I wouldn't put it past you," he added.

"Now I've got my legs again, I want to go skating and skiing. All the things I used to do."

"You've never done either," said David.

"Don't get technical," I said. "I want to go dancing in the moonlight."

"Now I know you're talking piss," said Marc. "You never could dance."

"Please be nice to me. It's the first day of the rest of my life."

"You've been watching too many bad films," said Marc.

"Humor me."

"Okay, baby, you shall go to the ball."

"That's a bit much, even for me."

"Whatever," said Marc. "I'm a bit over you walking, already."

"Actually, so am I."

"Have you had enough?" said David.

"I think so. It's exciting, but I'm tired."

Marc brought my wheelchair and gave me a tour of the sights he thought worthwhile. Then David took over and parked me in front of some ducks in a dirty pond. Eventually, they alternated pushing me back to the car. Alone in my flat, I walked from the living room into the kitchen and back, my hand against a wall, a door handle, the back of a sofa, anything that provided a little support. I went to bed that night feeling as though there might truly be an end to one of the worst periods of my life.

Part Three
Two Steps Forward

24

It wasn't as though I had to learn how to walk again; it was more a case of getting used to doing it with dodgy balance, coordination difficulties, and a reassembled leg. As soon as I managed this for a whole day without crutches, I went back to the gym. The first couple of times were exciting. It was something to do, and I had been so bored. By the third or fourth visit, it began to sink in how long full recovery might take. I was barely able to lift the lightest weight. People watched me with confusion or looked straight through me. To get to the toilet, I had to limp through the locker room, past men in various states of undress who turned away from me, indifferent. I felt ugly, useless, without sexual status. As usual, it was David who had to deal with this.

"Baby, you know how superficial this stuff is."

"That doesn't make it any less painful."

"You wanted to have a more natural body."

"It's different when the weight is taken from you."

"I can't believe it's getting to you."

"I wish I was mentally stronger, but I'm not."

"You don't fancy any of these men."

"I'd still like them to fancy me."

He laughed.

"I feel judged—and rejected."

"You're being hard on yourself. Everybody here is judged. It sounds like you're having to deal with reality again. Welcome back."

"Reality was like this? No wonder I never liked it."

David's statements struck a chord. What I felt in the gym was probably ancient stuff, the same insecurity and low self-esteem that had driven me there in the first place. I'd had a holiday in hospital—from vanity, superficiality, ego, sex, and arrogance. Something more elementary was always going on. Now I needed moral support as well as physical assistance.

My fifth workout was with a trainer I'd known for years, with whom I felt comfortable. We went slowly and I had a great session. He gave me plenty of rest, but by the time I got home I was exhausted. I undressed to take a bath, and out of habit looked in the hall mirror before getting in the tub. There was a difference. During my workout the trainer told me that muscles have memory, and that it probably wouldn't take long for me to get back in shape. Even though I'd heard this theory before, I'd dismissed it, thinking, *Yeah, right!* But now in my hall mirror, for the first time in so long, I could almost recognize my body as my own. Excited, I hurried my bath, then went into the living room to show David my new body. He smiled and told me that it looked lovely. I sat down next to him on the sofa, feeling good about my efforts and achievement.

"Do you mind?" I said, and pressed the remote for the TV. As the image came on, the phone rang.

"Hi, baby," came a voice.

"Who's that?" I said.

"What do you mean, 'Who's that?' It's your boyfriend."

"I didn't know I had one," I said. "Sorry, I mean I didn't expect you to call." Distracted by the inside of a womb on the screen, I added clumsily, "I mean, I wasn't expecting your call."

"Well, here I am," said Luke in a joking manner, as though we'd been speaking frequently.

"Luke, when I didn't hear from you, I decided not to care any more. I put your picture in the trash."

"You threw it away?"

"Yeah. It seemed odd having a picture of some guy I'd had sex with a bunch of times."

"Is that how you see it?"

"I don't know. No?"

"Good."

"I guess I just didn't feel like having you around any more. Not even the idea of you."

"I'm sorry I wasn't there for you when you needed me."

"So you knew it mattered to me?" I was silent for a moment, then said, "It's no big deal. I was okay, really," trying to make Luke feel better. But my mind said, *Whenever my hand needed holding, whenever I cried, whenever I was in pain or scared, David was here.*

"I'm sorry," said Luke.

"Don't misunderstand, I'd love to have spoken to you."

"I'd have called, but I was in the Redwoods."

"And before that?"

"In the mornings, I'd never remember. In the evenings, it was always too late."

"You could have called day or night."

"Are you mad at me?"

"Probably."

Luke was silent for a moment. "Do you not want to go out with me any more?"

"That's right."

"I could do with getting off the phone and having a cry."

"Do you mean that?"

"I don't want to lose you. I can't imagine not having you in my world."

"You don't have to," I said, confused. "I'm here if you need me, a phone call away."

"I love you," he said.

I paused. "Good night," was all I felt comfortable saying.

We hung up.

"Luke and I are through," I told David.

"You have been for a couple of months. It just took a while for you to realize it."

"In my own time," I said.

"I knew you could deal with it."

In bed that night, I wanted to call Luke, to see if he was okay. I distracted myself by wanking. The trouble was, images of Luke—most nonsexual, all compulsive—kept flashing in my mind. I'd manage to make him go away, then back he was, the battle continuing until I once again experienced that strange spasm that by now bored me. I wanted normality. I fell asleep quickly and slept soundly.

Most mornings I woke anxious at eight A.M., but that day I fell right back into a fairy-tale dream. I was under a sheet with Luke. We kissed. I sucked his dick and felt satisfied. (In the real world, I would have feared that one of us was getting bored.) Luke and I kissed again, a long time, both of us totally absorbed. I told Luke I loved him. As I started waking up, I clung to the dream, hoping to see what would happen next. But I could no longer keep reality at bay.

"Hado!" I shouted, looking at the time. It was ten o'clock.

"Hado, Sleeping Beauty," he replied.

On the way to the toilet, I stopped at the living room door. "Hado, again."

David looked up from his reading. "It *is* Sleeping Beauty."

"I bet," I said, pulling a face.

I continued to the toilet, still partially in the dream. Perhaps I didn't want to let go of Luke.

I made a cup of coffee and sat with David. "It's unlike me to sleep this late."

"Maybe you're feeling more relaxed."

"I dreamt about Luke."

"It's not surprising. You spoke to him before you went to bed."

"It was a beautiful dream."

"It makes sense that you'd idealize your relationship."

"It *was* ideal, sometimes."

"Like when you were in Miami?"

"No, cow face. I was thinking of other occasions."

"You seemed unhappy most of the time."

"Tell me I'm making the right decision."

"You didn't have much of a choice."

"It was perfect—the dream."

"It sounds like your dream was more real than your relationship ever was."

As usual, David was probably right.

25

After a few more workouts at the gym, my strength increased. I was happier with the way I looked, but it seemed the better I got physically, the less well I felt mentally. More out of reaching a benchmark than actual desire, I went to a nightclub. My old life was returning. At very least, a shabby version of it was coming into view.

I started going to nightclubs regularly. Like thousands of people all over the world, the only way I could face it was by getting high. Even by my standards, I took a lot of drugs (mainly acid, G, and K), hoping that doing so would make me more confident, less concerned with my appearance. Most ludicrous was that I hoped it would make other men less harsh in judging me. Predictably, drugs didn't do any of these things, and inevitably I sometimes took too many and David had to bring me home and put me to bed.

I couldn't see the point in living. I hoped the world would blow up. I took no pleasure in food, the sun, nighttime scents, men's bodies, laughing with friends. To make things worse, David found a buyer for his flat and quickly bought another he was keen to occupy. The day the movers came, I went to the gym, thinking it would be less traumatizing than having loud, unfamiliar men in my home.

I returned to an empty, bleak apartment. Dust marks showed where David's things had been. My TV had stopped working. Repairmen came and took it away to be fixed. What would I do by myself? How would I spend the long evenings? I'd never felt more scared and miserable.

I began taking sleeping tablets every night. Finally I asked my doctor to prescribe antidepressants. He also referred me to a therapist who specialized in trauma cases. I quite enjoyed my sessions, but didn't find them that useful.

The antidepressants were another matter. At first, I became sleepless, like I was on speed, and found myself grinding my teeth. After about three weeks, I was smiling all the time, as though I'd had my jaw wired into a grin. I even laughed. At the same time, I felt such sadness.

Crossing the road became easier. I'd got used to standing on the pavement and waiting for traffic to clear. In a city as busy as London, this can take ages. If it was rush hour, I'd have to go blocks out of my way to a light, it being the only pedestrian crossing drivers take seriously. Now, if one side was clear, I was able to walk to the middle of the road—even if hard, fast, previously threatening traffic rushed behind me—and wait for the other side to clear. Progress, if chemically induced.

I felt able to face things I'd been putting off, like my appointment to have a wisdom tooth removed. The roots were so bent, my mouth had to be cut open to get at them. More worrying was that part of the root wrapped around nerves. My first appointment had been for the week after my coming out of hospital, and I couldn't face it. The new one arrived quickly enough. David drove me to the appointment and came into the office with me, then sat in front of me, smiling, as I was fitted with a bright orange plastic bib. Aware of how silly it looked, I tucked it into my shorts. Adding insult to injury, the nurse handed me one-size-fits-all green plastic goggles. I posed, propping my chin on the back of my hand.

"How do I look?" I asked David.

"Very modern, but somehow eighteenth century."

I changed position and gave him a cheesy smile.

"Very handsome," said the nurse.

"Very catalogue model," said David.

I straightened my goggles and pretended to act cool.

"Could you open your mouth nice and wide now, Mr. Shaw?" said the dentist.

"Are you expecting much mess?" I asked, referring to the outfit.

The dentist smiled.

"I think that's a yes," said David.

"I've had my fill of surgery this year," I said. "Please go easy."

"I'm sure Dr. Kundo will do the best he can," said the nurse. I believe she meant to reassure me.

Dr. Kundo gave me eight injections in the mouth. After about twenty minutes, he got to work, and put so much pressure on my head that the nurse had to support it.

He pulled back. "Does it hurt?" he said.

"No, but it feels like my head might come off."

"Don't worry," said the nurse. "I'll catch it."

I opened my mouth once more, and focused on David, wiggling my fingers at him (all I could manage, my arms being trapped by the weight of the bodies on either side of me). Finally, after weird noises I never expected to hear coming from my head, the ugliest tooth was held inches from my face. I was fascinated, if not disgusted, that it had been part of me.

David suggested I keep it. The nurse washed it and put it in a plastic bag for me. Prescription for antibiotics and painkillers in hand, I left the dentist's feeling assaulted. David drove me home.

That night, sleep came easily again. Pleasant dreams in which activities still not possible, like running—nothing too ambitious, just enough to make me feel like things were improving—were now routine. Once, I dreamt I was kissing the eyelids of some lovely, unknown boy, who liked my doing it.

I came off sleeping tablets, cut down on melatonin, and decreased my dose of antidepressants by half, planning to stop taking them completely. My doctor prescribed testosterone to help me gain weight. It did much more than that. It made me feel rejuvenated, vital—and very horny. I felt more like my old self, independent and confident. David said I even looked different. Familiar. (His actual words were, "I remember you.")

Facing my HIV again, I had blood work done. To my surprise, my T4 cells were at an all-time high and my viral load at an all-time low. I'd never seen my doctor so optimistic. I tried not to let this affect my mood, but the first thing I did when I got home was call my mum, who had been concerned when I'd missed a week's medication in Brussels in intensive care. She was delighted with the news. She'd spent a week at Lourdes, referred to my recovery as miraculous, and was still having daily masses said for me. I thought it wasn't miraculous that I'd got run over in the first place.

I phoned Luke, telling myself it was to maintain some semblance of friendship. When he didn't pick up, I called Nina, hoping to distract myself, but it wasn't long before the conversation centered on Luke.

"Maybe he's out of town," she said, and paused.

"What are you thinking?" I said.

"I can't believe you haven't asked him for your mother's ring back."

"I couldn't." If it didn't remind him that he loved me, I wanted it to remind him of some kind of love. At least it would be seen. "I'd rather he had it than it be sitting in my drawer. It's a beautiful ring."

"You think he still wears it? He's probably sold it by now."

"No! Do you think?"

"It's more probable than likely."

"Nobody's that heartless."

"Right," she said. "In whose reality?"

Nina's accusations silenced me. Gracefully, she let me get off the phone. I kept the receiver in my hand, as though about to make another call. I guess I hadn't yet heard what I wanted to hear.

The living room window was open and the air was packed with smells, sparking memories. My mind drifted. I had a vague notion that I could see some point to living again. I pulled myself back to the present, thinking, *Fuck that—fuck him.* I made a cup of coffee to wake myself before going to therapy, where I was due in less than an hour.

Partly to show my therapist I could but more to show myself, the new me decided to try riding my bicycle to the session. I wheeled it out the front door. The ground was dry; there shouldn't be any problem. I climbed on, standing on my good leg and lifting my left leg over. I sat, pushed forward, and wobbled down the ramp leading from my building. This was only to be expected; it would be okay. I rode through the court-yard, barely able to balance or keep to a straight line. Memories of when I was a kid came back to me: clowns riding tiny bikes in crooked lines, how silly they looked. I pulled cautiously onto the road, which luckily was clear. For some reason, I was unable to straighten up. I knew what I wanted to do, but the bike seemed to have a mind of its own.

In an instant the road was full of cars. I kept my eyes forward, not knowing if I was able to turn my head enough to look behind me. It felt as though I'd never ridden a bike before. What should have been natural and easy was awkward and perilous. Anxiety rushed through me. The cars seemed close, dangerous, the upcoming intersection so busy. I decided to get off and wheel the bike across. I stopped, tentatively leaning to my left toward the pavement, away from traffic. But my leg wasn't where it was meant to be. Seemingly disconnected from my brain, it folded under the bike. Tipping, I fell.

Should I try to lift myself with my left arm? Surely it wouldn't work properly, either. Cars sped by. I decided it would be safer to try with my right hand. As though doing push-ups, I lifted myself and dragged my legs, scuttling crablike from under the bike. No one came to help me or asked how I was. Finally up, I dusted myself off. Then, out of confusion or embarrassment rather than amusement, I burst out laughing. People did seem to notice this. I was beyond caring.

Commending myself, I wheeled the bike back to my flat. Before setting off again, I had just enough time to call David and tell him what happened. He assumed the mishap had upset me, and responded with concern. I reassured him that I was okay about it. I arrived for my session slightly flustered, and recounted my mishap to my therapist. The best he could come up with was to ask how the experience made me feel. We killed thirty-five minutes with his asking questions and my making jokes before he finally said, "How do you want to spend the next twenty-five minutes?"

"You don't normally ask me how I want to do therapy," I said. "We just do it."

"Yes, but it seems there isn't anything in particular to talk about."

"Are you referring to the accident?"

"Well, yes."

"I admit, the accident is becoming less significant, but you make it sound as though we're through."

"Do you think there is anything more to cover?"

"Of course."

"Like what?"

"Where do I begin? We could talk about my low self-esteem, and possibly my BIDS."

"Do you have Body Image Distortion?"

"I hope so. If I really am how I think I am, then God help me."

"How do you see yourself?"

"Are we starting this now?"

"We could," he said.

"Or?"

"Or have a couple of weeks break, then start."

"I like the sound of that," I said. "I'm feeling so different every day. In two weeks, things may have settled down a little."

26

A nightclub called Heaven asked Whatever to perform at their midweek "alternative night." We weren't keen on playing gay venues; the audiences didn't care who was onstage unless they were pop stars. But we thought the midweek crowd might be more interested—or at least want to appear to be—and it was an opportunity for me to face my fears about performing. We agreed to do it.

Like many things in my life, whether being filmed fucking some model's ass, sitting on a punter's face, or having Christmas dinner with my family, doing a gig was partly about accepting that I was capable of doing it, and partly just pretending I could. The Heaven gig was no different. I acted as though I was Aiden Shaw doing a concert with his kooky art-house band. I sang, posed, spoke a bit, moved around the stage acting sexy, punky, cool. The audience seemed none the wiser, but equally I'm sure, most didn't give a damn. Despite this, our set went much better than we'd expected. Nothing went drastically wrong.

In our dressing room afterward we greeted friends, many of whom I hadn't seen for a long time, and I got drunk on the free drinks supplied by the club. As Nina and I popped an E, Heaven closed. We collected our friends and adjourned to an unlicensed after-hours bar in Chinatown where straight dealers stood side by side with queers, rough, unglamorous transsexuals of the old school, and anyone else who hadn't had enough yet. It reminded me of bars I'd gone to when I was a teenager, in the days when queens were harder-faced and nights never seemed complete until someone was bottled, or at least thrown down some stairs.

We bought cocaine and went in groups to the toilet. The intimacy of the cubicles sometimes offered the only chance in a club to talk to people properly, a quiet moment away from sensory pollution. Back in the main room, we all set about using our coked-up state, speaking lots of rubbish peppered with brilliant jokes, intriguing slang, and the obligatory exchange of false sentiment along with some genuine old-friend insight and warmth.

One of the dealers began an ambiguous conversation with me, filled with obscure innuendo. Slowly it dawned that he wanted me and one of my girlfriends to go home with him. He was very handsome, a big guy with black-brown skin, a shaved head, and lips that looked like they were talking about fucking no matter what they actually said. Not wanting to miss an opportunity to act up, show off, and see how far we could go, I asked Nina if she was interested. She, of course, said yes.

Soon we were heading toward Shepherd's Bush, the dealer sitting between us in the cab. Before long, his sweatpants were down and Nina and I alternated giving him head. (It was a minicab, so there was no division between the driver and us. Like all good cabbies, he didn't seem fazed by our behavior.) At the dealer's house, we stripped naked, except for Nina, who left on her seamless tights, which she wore without underpants. She looked amazing and she knew it.

The dealer moved a chest of drawers in front of the door to make sure nobody else came in the room. Apparently, there were other people in the house, although it seemed quiet and still. We smoked all the dealer's drugs, surprised at how little he had for a pro. We suspected he was plying us with crack, not cocaine. (I never could tell them apart, and it wasn't as though Nina or I cared, anyway.) We took turns doing various things to the dealer, careful not to touch each other. Sharing this man with Nina felt like sharing a tasty meal. It was almost like we were giving each other pleasure without crossing the unique boundaries established in our relationship.

Inevitably, I had to pee. Rather than deal with the chest of drawers, the dealer suggested I go in a bottle he handed me.

"Don't waste that," said Nina. Seeing my response, she rolled her eyes and said, "The *bottle*, not the piss."

"I know," I lied.

"Here," she said, handing me a pint glass, "use this."

We swapped bottle and glass, and I set about peeing. When I was done, I looked up to find Nina crouched over the dealer's face, pushing the bottle in her cunt.

"Is that nice?" I said.

"I prefer Coca-Cola," said Nina.

"You guys are too much," said the dealer.

"It's better than not enough," I said.

"Sure is," he agreed, his eyes riveted on the bottle.

I took a moment to freeze-frame the scene in memory, then joined them. As we continued our coked-up version of sex, I started to come down from my drugs.

"I've had enough," I said to Nina.

"What does that mean?" she replied.

"It's when the drugs have really, really, really run out."

"Oh, you mean there isn't enough?"

"That's right."

"Are there no more drugs at all?" she asked the dealer, an innocent look on her face.

"I can go get some," he said.

"In that case," said Nina, "*I'll* stay."

"It was hit-and-miss there for a while," I said.

"Yeah, like a nanosecond," said Nina. "I'm cunted now, I may as well have fun with it."

But I had to leave. The dealer offered to walk out with me, moving the chest of drawers while I dressed. Nina sat beside me on the bed as I tied my laces, studying me with the best version of concern and an appropriate half smile possible at that time of the morning, after that many drugs.

"You okay?"

"I'm sorry, baby," I said. "I've got to take my meds."

"No problem."

With a final heave, the chest of drawers cleared the door. I thought vaguely of a rock and something biblical. Almost as quickly as Nina and I had got them off, the dealer pulled on his sweatpants.

"Ready?"

"Yep." Looking Nina in the eye, I said, "Are you sure you want to stay?"

"Yeah. Don't worry, petal. I'm a big girl."

"Yeah," said the dealer. "She can look after herself, mate."

Nina raised her eyebrows comically in a way that could have meant anything, from *Shut up and deal* to *Like you give a damn.*

Reassured by her awareness of the situation, I said good-bye and we gave each other a long hug full of protection and acceptance. It was the most physical contact we'd had all evening, possibly the most communicative, definitely the most heartfelt.

27

Our next gig was at the Kitten Club in Camden Town. We'd booked it previously, but had to cancel because I was still in hospital. Doing the gig now signaled that the whole episode was over. Besides, we'd invited a management company to see us perform.

I'd written a new song we'd rehearsed almost to boredom. The sound check went fine and, feeling confident at least about this, we went for dinner. Obviously still nervous, I was unable to chew or swallow, though the red wine went down easily enough. Afterward we went to Nina's, because she lived nearby. There we continued to drink and prepared ourselves for the evening ahead with our time-honored tradition, both mystical and profound, of doing two or three lines of cocaine and talking nonsense. This didn't make me any less nervous, but it gave me something else to think about. Finally we were ready and set off to the club.

We continued to talk loudly and hear nothing in the cab, Nina holding my hand all the way. As we entered the Kitten Club, a man stopped me, professing to be from the management company we'd invited. This should have made me even more nervous, but to a certain extent I was already onstage, and therefore oblivious to anybody but Nina and Marc. We told the soundman we were ready, and within minutes began the show.

Nina and Marc were in their element onstage, both fabulous and cool. For me, seeing people I liked in the audience was the most rewarding part of doing a concert. I spotted some friends dancing next to the stage looking like they were having a great time, as well as my brother Des. At one point, a woman reached up and handed me a flower, then pulled me down and kissed me. I put the flower on my microphone stand. Next she passed me a little brown bottle—GHB I guessed by the smell of it, and undiluted. I took a swig, using beer as a chaser.

My new song was the last in our set. Nina and Marc sang the first line, I sang the second, and so forth.

Yeah, yeah, yeah
I know your face
Yeah, yeah, yeah
It was at your place
Yeah, yeah, yeah
It's been a long time
Yeah, yeah, yeah
Such a sometime
Yeah, yeah, yeah
We had fun
Yeah, yeah, yeah
A little more than humdrum

The next section was spoken by me, with Marc and Nina doing whatever they liked. Marc would sometimes sing choirboy-like backup, and Nina would sometimes address what I'd said. Tonight they did both.

> We walked a while
> We talked a while
> We ate
> We drank
> We smiled
> We stared a while
> We shared a while
> We danced
> We laughed
> Got high
> I stayed a while
> You stayed a while
> We slept
> We woke
> We smoked
> We lived a while
> We loved a while
> We played around
> Got bored

Next, I sang the first line, Nina and Marc the second, and so on.

> I've never seen such lips before
> Never seen. Never seen
> Never seen such lips before
> Never seen. I've never seen

Just me:

> Kiss me kiss me kiss me, will you
> Kiss me kiss me kiss me, will you

My Undoing

Kiss me kiss me kiss me, will you
Kiss me kiss me kiss me
Please

Then, as before:

Yeah, yeah, yeah

And:

Walking. Talking.
I thought that you liked me
Staring. Sharing.
Getting so fucked up
Sleeping. Waking.
God, I used to love that
Living. Loving.
What was the name again?

I've never seen such lips before
Never seen, I've never seen
I've never seen such lips before
Never seen, I've never seen

Kiss me kiss me kiss me, will you
Kiss me kiss me kiss me, will you
Kiss me kiss me kiss me, will you
Kiss me kiss me kiss me, will you

Yeah, yeah, yeah
I know your face
Yeah, yeah, yeah
It was at your place
Yeah, yeah, yeah

It's been a long time
Yeah, yeah, yeah
Such a sometime
Yeah, yeah, yeah
We had fun
Yeah, yeah, yeah
A little more than humdrum

The song shows my confusion about Luke, and my subsequent cynicism. Regardless, it went down well, and the gig as a whole was one of our best ever. Even Des, ordinarily impossible to please, enjoyed the set. Later, the manager cornered me at the bar.

"You guys were fantastic," he said.

"You're just saying that because you want to work with us," I said.

"I'm not, but I do."

"Really?" I shouted down the bar. "Nina, come here!"

To avoid losing her place, she slid along the bar toward us. "What, precious?" she said, turning her head but keeping one eye on the barman.

"This geezer is from some management company, and he wants to work with us."

Nina flicked a glance at him, checking him out, pulled out a pen, wrote down her number, handed it to him without looking, and said, "Give me a call tomorrow."

"Sure," he said. "The name's Sid, by the way."

"Great!" She turned back toward the bar. After a pause, she turned to us again, only slightly, and said to me, "Drink, baby?"

"Whatever," I said.

Getting the barman's attention, she said, "Two double vodkas and Coke, please." Then, quickly, to me: "One whatever coming up."

We continued drinking until the Kitten Club closed for the night, then went with the people who ran it to a party where I drank, laughed, got higher, and finally decided to go home. My bag was hidden in the bathroom. When I tried to retrieve it, the door was locked. I knocked; the door opened a crack. Nina's face appeared. I could see a thin line of her naked body.

"Sorry for disturbing you, baby, but my bag's in the cupboard behind you."

She closed the door, then returned with the bag. "Are you going?" she said.

"Yeah. Are you having fun?"

"Yeah," she said, pulling a face that meant *not really*. "I'm with a wallet."

"That's handy. Are you sure you're okay?"

"Definitely."

"I'll leave you to it, then."

"Bye."

"You were brilliant tonight, baby," I said.

"*You* were," she said. "Well done."

I looked her in the eye and said, "I love you."

"Yeah, yeah, yeah," she said, poking her head turtle-like through the crack. Then she kissed me, smiled what I knew to be a genuine smile, and closed the door.

28

What with rehearsing, performing, and anxiety over new gigs, my mind was pretty occupied—or preoccupied. Physically, I was becoming more able-bodied all the time; physiologically, I didn't really feel prone to depression. Clearly, I was getting my life back. I was too grateful to wonder if I wanted it to be the *old* one. I decided to stop taking antidepressants.

Two days after playing the Kitten Club, we were on our way to Heathrow and our next gig: headlining at the Castro Street Fair in San Francisco. Paul, a boy Marc had started seeing, drove us to the airport. Their good-bye was unhurried and reluctant; Nina and I waited, barely patient.

No matter what time you arrive at check-in, there is always a queue. Nina and Marc were about to join the line when I told them "I'm on the guest list." During my years doing porn in the States, I'd flown so much that I'd become a premier frequent flyer, which entitled me and whoever was with me to check in at the business class section. A good-looking

Frenchman ticketed us, much to the annoyance of a snooty woman next in line who clearly thought we were trash.

(We'd all made a special effort to disguise ourselves and fit in, dressing up in smart and casual airplane clothes. I'd parted my hair on the side, wore a button-up shirt, and generally looked as though I'd made different choices in life and not become the person I actually was. Nina looked like somebody's studious sister who worked in the local library. Marc had somehow dressed both up and down, concealing his blue hair with beige mousse. The result was kind of not-colored-in, a little like a drag queen out of makeup or the punter's flat in Miami. Something like this always seemed to give us away, and the *real* people could tell we were impostors.)

"Are these business class?" said the annoyed woman in a weary voice. The Frenchman looked up from his work and said, "Yes, madam. If you'd like to wait your turn, somebody will be with you shortly." Marc and I smiled at each other. I quietly thanked the Frenchman. "It's nothing," he said. "She's very rude." He shook our hands and wished us a great trip. I'd never had such pleasant service.

U.S. Customs went surprisingly smoothly, and we were met by a white stretch limousine. It was embarrassingly tacky, but so spacious Nina could lie down fully and I was able to stretch out my legs in the back, amenities much appreciated after the long, cramped international flight. Marc sat next to the driver, staring out the front window, the only one not tinted. No matter how many times I've been to San Francisco, its prettiness never ceases to impress me. It looked like Marc and Nina were being similarly affected.

We were taken to the apartment of a man called Lavern, who had given us his flat for the duration. Lavern had put himself in charge of looking after us. He had bleached blond hair with gray roots, stank of cigarettes, and spoke with a strange accent he must have thought sounded French. His clothes were too small for him. He wore large nipple rings, which protruded through his mesh top. I wondered what decade his head was in, and what reality. (He looked like he'd stepped out of the 1970s, but without any retro coolness.) His apartment had a shrine to the recently deceased Princess Diana, with many pictures of her, a Buddha, candles, incense—and pictures of me, including stills from videos and press photos. Nina, Marc, and I gathered around the shrine, aghast. Nina sighed, Marc rolled his eyes. I felt spooked, but said only, "How precious. A princess shrine."

We turned in early. Marc wanted to sleep on the futon on the floor, which he felt would be better for his back. I brushed my teeth and got into bed beside Nina.

"Can I cuddle you?" she said.

I couldn't help smiling, "Why do you think I chose the bed?"

"Which way do you want to face?"

"Do you have a preference?"

"I like to curl around people."

"Okay," I said.

Nina held me. "Men never hold me like this," I said. It felt good.

"It takes a woman like me to hold a man like you."

"Now you tell me."

"You've been hanging with the wrong crowd," she said, and kissed the back of my neck.

"Who, men?"

"If you don't get what you need."

As a rule, with men my needs didn't break through their fantasy of me. I could shout, "I want to be held" and it would fall on deaf ears. Presumably, I encouraged this, or they didn't want to hear. I fell asleep amid confused thoughts about role-playing and cozy feelings for Nina. It had been a good day.

Lavern had arranged dinner for us the next evening. It felt like a special occasion, and we all made an effort with our clothes. Nina and I linked arms on the way. Our friend Rifat Ozbeck, a fashion designer, had given her a dress he'd made, and I'm sure he would have thought she wore it well. She looked elegant, severe, and sexy. Everybody who passed us on the street turned to look at her as she walked by.

The restaurant staff gave us their best table, pampering us thoroughly. A live light-jazz band provided unintrusive entertainment. The food was just right, and we drank three or four bottles of wine before returning to Lavern's apartment satiated. I fell asleep relaxed and happy, without a trace of pre-gig anxiety.

The sound check, scheduled for ten A.M., didn't happen until nearly eleven. Afterward we had a late breakfast at Café Flore, on Market Street, then made our way back to the apartment. It was October, but the sun shone like summer. A crisp quality to the air made it feel like the first day of a brand new world. Crowds of people were already gathered near the corner of Castro and Market.

We bathed and got ready, our excitement building, then ran through the set a couple of times and took pictures of each other with a disposable camera. Marc loaned me a T-shirt to wear onstage, and once I'd donned it spent a long time meticulously drawing thick red veins on my arms. They expressed how I felt: vulnerable, as though I had no protective skin. An open wound.

Lavern's apartment was only a few blocks from Castro Street, and we decided to walk to the stage. Along the way, we took more photographs. I needed help negotiating the steep hills, which Nina anticipated and provided. (It seemed second nature to her to support and care for me like this—perhaps because she'd grown up with a sister who had MS and a mother with MRSA.) When we arrived at the fair, we hung around behind the stage, drinking lager. Nina and I did some cocaine in one of the Port-a-Loos. Before we knew it, we were being introduced.

Tired of having to balance onstage, I'd asked for a chair to sit on or lean against and basically treat as a crutch. Lavern had given us three: a simple metal chair for Marc, who worked it like a pro (at one point, I think he even spun it on one leg); and a wicker chair for Nina, with a huge dovetail backrest and the grubby dirty-white residue of an old paint job (nasty; the only interaction she had with the chair was to snub it—I swear she even gave it attitude). My chair was actually a tall stool, easy to deal with: I simply sat on it.

Assuming Luke was in the audience, I introduced a song I'd written especially for him, "Unrealistic Lover," which I sang to plain acoustic guitar accompaniment, Nina and Marc backing me with dulcet harmonies.

Maybe it's too much to want
Someone to fill every need
To teach
Inspire
And be told
To touch
To kiss
And to hold

Maybe it's too hard to find
Someone who's open and kind
To listen
Comfort
And share
To laugh
Encourage
And care

Someone wise
Who knows what he has to offer

My Undoing

Someone strong
Who knows what I want
Someone
Or something
That knows everything
Like God
And I could live as a baby
Being loved
And loved
And loved
No need
No more want
No more waiting
Oh how sweet a thing

I want to belong to this
Someone wise
To this
Someone strong
Someone
Or something
That knows everything
Like God
So he'll ring on my phone
Knock on my door
Or fly through my window tonight
And love me
Love me
Love
No need
No more want
No more waiting
Oh how sweet a thing

We headed off to the backstage area and found people waiting behind the barrier imploring me to come sign autographs and take pictures with them.

Marc tapped me on the shoulder. "Luke's here."

I turned. He was standing some distance from us, behind the barrier. I gestured to him that I would be finished in a minute. But every time I tried to break away, somebody called me back. In my peripheral vision I saw Luke leaving. He seemed annoyed. I looked at him. I told the people waiting for autographs I'd be back in a moment, then walked as quickly as I could, managing to cut Luke off at the far side of the backstage area, where I apologized for taking so long to get to him. He leaned over the barrier as though flirting with a stranger, smiled his lazy smile, and said, "I'm still waiting for you to return my call."

The sunlight caught the small blond hairs on his shoulders. I was careful not to get too close; part of me wanted to move in and kiss him. I tried to see beyond his sunglasses, but was distracted by a memory of us naked together. After a moment, I said softly, "Luke, I've got to ask you something everyone always asks me. Where were you?"

"I've told you. I went to the Redwoods."

"Why?"

"It had been planned."

"I was in a wheelchair."

"What was I supposed to do, sit at home sulking?"

"Fucking yeah!"

Clearly he didn't care, which anyone could have told me as far back as Miami. My fantasy had been more important than the reality. It took this moment to make me finally stop fooling myself. Deep inside, I said my final good-bye to Luke. I couldn't look at him any longer. I turned and headed back to Marc and Nina. Knowing people were watching us, Luke twisted his mouth into a smile and waved.

I sat on the ramp leading to the stage. The crowd of people waiting for autographs had grown. They shouted my name. I put my head in my hands and cried.

When I fell in love with Luke, it wasn't specifically with him. I'd wanted to fall in love, and anybody who looked the part, said the right things, would do. I think my crying now wasn't about Luke either, but about my accident, and probably many things prior to that. Luke symbolized all the hurt I'd ever connected with. The only really surprising thing was that I ever stopped crying.

"Bastard," said Marc. "Did you see him when we were onstage?"

"No," I said.

"Good. He was standing near the front, hanging off some boy."

I'd noticed Marc and Nina conferring as I performed a solo during "Unrealistic Lover." "Is that what you and Nina were talking about?" I asked now.

"Yeah. I hoped you wouldn't see him." Marc looked angry.

"What can we do, baby?" said Nina.

"Don't worry, I'm fine. Just answer this: Why?"

"Because he's young," said Marc.

"No. I mean why would somebody bring tear gas to a concert?"

Nina chuckled politely. Sensing I was okay, she said, "What do you want to do now?"

"Honestly?"

"Always honestly, I hope."

"Get really fucked up."

They both laughed.

"That's my boy!" said Marc.

"What are we waiting for?" said Nina.

Within minutes, back at the apartment, we had smoked, snorted, and swallowed every bit of crystal, cocaine, Ecstasy, Special K, hash, and acid we could lay our hands on. I can't remember ever doing so many drugs in such a short time. Hours passed like seconds. We headed out to 1015, where we were on the guest list. At the door of the club I bumped into Cliff Parker, the man in the porn video the Miami-dog-paw-bottle-punter had shown me. Cliff's real name was Ron. His eyes twinkled, his face glowed. I could feel happiness coming off him, and I wanted it.

"My God, you look beautiful," I said.

"So do you."

The door area was congested; we had to move constantly. "Where are you going?" I said.

"Home."

He was actually leaving early (he felt sick), but I had lost all sense of time. "Can I give you my number?" I said.

"Sure. I'll give you mine, too."

Neither of us had anything to write with, and neither of us was in a fit state to get it. But I didn't want to lose contact with Ron. Sensing my plight, the woman on the door held up a pen. I smiled. Numbers swapped, I felt happier about letting Ron go. I kissed him. He returned the gesture.

"Excuse me," somebody said. We were blocking the door. Ron and I stepped aside to let people by, keeping hold of each other's hands. "Aiden!" urged a voice from inside the club sounding like someone calling me to dinner for the umpteenth time. Ron gave me one more sparkling smile, then left.

The men on the dance floor at 1015 could have been having lots of fun; maybe they even had personality, individuality, depth. All I could see were muscular men with no shirts on. Eventually, I took one of them home with me. After sex, I used some pathetic excuse to get him to leave. It required fifty milligrams of Valium and four sleeping tablets before I could sleep. (It was already lunchtime a day later, and it would be a long time before the crystal I'd taken let me sleep naturally.) Before I shut off completely, I left a message on Ron's answering machine. About five hours later I woke up and called him again. He invited me to hang out at his place.

"I don't think I'm fit to be seen," I said. "I'm half vegetable."

"What's the other half?"

"That's the problem. There isn't one."

"That's the way I like them," he said, and offered to come get me.

But first Marc turned up, planning to take the same bunch-of-downers route to sleep I had, and told me Nina had gone out looking for adventure, or at least somewhere she could stay awake all day. Midway through a description of some trip to the bar at 1015, Marc was unconscious.

I was pottering about neurotically when I heard the deep, soft rumble of Ron's motorbike pulling up outside. I quickly checked that I had everything I needed—toothbrush, pocket telephone book, sleeping tablets—then made my way downstairs. Ron wore a leather jacket and looked wonderful leaning against his bike. He smiled diffidently and said hello. We opted for a hug as greeting; although we'd once spent a day fucking on film, we were both self-conscious about how physical we should or shouldn't be now. At the same time, I got the impression we were both somewhat embarrassed by not knowing how to behave in "real life." I distracted us by asking enthusiastic, inane questions about Ron's bike. Like a sexy cowboy, he mounted his saddle and handed me a helmet. I climbed on behind him, placing my hands around his waist. As we rode they progressed under his T-shirt to his hairy tummy. Very sexy.

The evening was mild, the ride to Ron's apartment gorgeous. The first thing I did when we got there was lie down. Ron went for a blanket and placed it beside me.

"In case you get cold."

"What are you for, then?" I said, pulling him by the hand down next to me.

"Do you like *The Simpsons*?" he said.

"Do I like *The Simpsons*? *Ai, caramba!*"

Ron started singing, "Fi, fi, fi. Fi, fi, fi." I joined in: "*The Itchy and Scratchy Show.*"

We spent the evening on his sofa. Ron ordered Chinese food, then ran me a bath and kept me company, sitting on the edge of the tub. By ten o'clock I was wiped out, and asked if I could get into bed. (I assumed it was okay to stay over.) He seemed only too happy to lead me to the bedroom.

I heard rainfall. "What's that?" I said. "I love it."

"A sound machine." Ron tucked me in.

"How old are you?" I said.

"Thirty-one, why?"

"I'm not used to someone I fancy looking after me."

"Get used to it." Ron kissed the side of my head. "I've got some chores to do. I'll come in when I'm finished."

"If I'm asleep, don't be scared to wake me."

"You don't scare me."

The sound machine was perfect for someone obsessive as myself. I drifted into a semidream state, thinking, *Falling rain. Oh, it's the sound machine*—and recalling how falling rain made me feel as a child looking out the window, happily watching and listening. Ten minutes later I'd think, *Falling rain. Oh, it's the sound machine* again—and recall another memory. I don't know how long this continued.

"Hey, you," I half heard. "Do you want anything?"

Ron lay behind me in bed, holding me. I roused myself to answer, "Yes, you," then woke up enough to have sex.

Soon after we started, Ron said, "Why don't you open your eyes?"

"I'm sorry. I've learned to keep them shut."

"Why?"

"Some people think it's creepy if you look at them during sex."

"Do you think it's creepy?"

"I love it."

"So do I."

Looking directly at each other we kissed, and now that I allowed my eyes to be open I took a good look at Ron. He was remarkable, a perfect specimen of what, as a child, I'd dreamt men might be. The sight of him made me horny, let alone feeling his hairy body rubbing against mine. I pigged out.

Ron was the ideal lover—receptive, responsive, reciprocating, as affectionate as a child. He seemed less self-orientated, more adult than most of the men I'd been with. Eventually, we settled down to sleep.

"Turn around," said Ron.

"I usually go on the outside."

"Not tonight."

"Why?"

"You seem like you need holding."

"Just like that?"

"Why not?"

"I thought it was about playing roles."

"Not with me. When I need holding, I'll let you know."

"How modern."

"Turn around."

We swapped positions many times that night. It made me wonder why I ever put up with anything else.

When we awoke, Ron took me back to Lavern's apartment to see Nina and Marc. They were happy doing their own thing, Marc determined to go swimming, Nina to catch up on all the sleep she'd missed.

The next day, our last in San Francisco, Ron drove me north on his bike. The sun on my back, the sound of the gulls, the smell of the ocean, the view along the coast were thrilling. I held on tight to Ron, stroking his tummy with my fingers. His back warmed my front and the inside of my thighs, giving me a hard-on. Resting my chin on his shoulder, I saw in his wing mirror a man in a half helmet, the sun reflecting off his dark glasses. I smiled at him and he smiled back. I'd been in a deep pit, becoming bitter, jaded, angry. Ron offered me his hand, making me see things another way. I was grateful. Later we drove through Golden Gate Park, pulling into Ron's street with just enough time to have sex before meeting Nina and Marc for dinner.

Ron and I arrived at the restaurant first. When the others turned up, they greeted us with kisses. I noticed that Marc looked different—serious, distracted. When we sat down he slipped something small and hard into my palm the way a dealer hands over drugs in a club, feigning discretion but making it obvious to anybody what's actually going on. I lifted my hand, opened it, and couldn't believe my eyes.

"I went round with Nina," explained Marc.

"What did you say?"

"'I want the ring back.'"

"Is that all?"

"I didn't really feel like chatting," said Marc.

"I did," said Nina. "I told him he was a callous cunt."

"Graphic visual," said Ron.

"What did he say?" I asked.

"He didn't agree."

"That sounds like Luke," I said. "Remote. Anyway, I can't believe this."

"Fucking right," said Ron. "What great friends."

"Hear, hear," I said, lifting my glass. I reached for Marc's hand and slid the ring on his finger.

"Finally!" said Marc. "I've always loved this ring."

"Now it can love you, too."

He smiled, which made me smile. No matter how generous a spirit I wanted to pretend I had, or how benevolent I aspired to be about Luke, it felt right that he no longer had my mum's engagement ring. It felt even more right that Marc did. My mum had always liked him. When calling me, he was the only person besides David she always asked after. I believed knowing Marc had her ring would make her smile as well.

29

One day when I was grown up and living on my own, my mother told me that I'd always been her favorite child. It was odd hearing her put in words what I'd always thought to be the case; parents aren't supposed to admit such things. Another time, she casually mentioned my being gay—and said it meant that I'd never leave her, apparently thinking of the old adage that daughters are for life but sons are only yours until they get married. It touched me deeply that my mum had taken what some parents would consider a negative revelation and turned it into something positive. Other little things indicated that our relationship was special. She'd show me clothes she'd made and I'd know the difference between a skirt and a dress—nothing too technical, really, but many straight men (my father especially) never manage to figure it out. When buying a birthday present, I knew what her favorite perfume was—all it took was a casual remark about how good she smelled to crack that mystery. And she wasn't the only one to benefit; it worked both ways. Whenever I have relationship problems, my mum is the person I turn to for advice; nobody else I know has been with a partner over forty years. She always has an apt anecdote about how she and my father dealt with a situation that happened to them that makes me feel I'm not a freak. She never lets me down.

As for what she knows about my life in the sex industry, my mum is highly skilled at extracting what information she wants and disregarding elements she doesn't need. She knew older men gave me money for spending time with them, and thought them kind and me special that people would do this. In order for her to be able to show off my published novels to her friends, she had me supply her with foreign editions of which they wouldn't be able to read even the cover copy. My favorite example of this sort of thing came in the early 1990s when I was frequently on the cover of *Torso* or *Honcho* or *Inches* or some other American gay skin magazine. I sent her one of them—I can't remember which—and she removed the cover, folded back the edges, concealed any remaining print with a colored pen matching the background, then framed it and hung it in the dining room next to a photograph of Cardinal Hulme holding my nephew in Westminster Cathedral!

So I wasn't entirely surprised when, the day after my return to London, a package from my mum arrived in the post. Not quite awake yet, I opened it expecting to find clothing. I was partly right; inside was a sweatshirt, but wrapped around something else: a miniature replica of Michelangelo's *Pietà*. I was dragged back to my childhood, to a hectic house filled with the smell of washing powder and cooking food, and sounds of vacuum cleaning and reprimands. There were lots of children: two girls and five boys. Fights broke out several times a day—my father worked too often away from home (hardly surprising). My mum was barely able to cope. I suspect the only thing that got her through was her profound belief in God. She encouraged us kids to believe, too, and for a while I did. I even had a little figure of Jesus I knelt and prayed to every night before bed, convinced he was kind, sweet, forgiving. In time, I stopped. Now I can't help thinking I only carried out this ritual because it was a particularly handsome statue and I always loved kissing men. (I could go so far as to say I worship them.) Something of Mum did rub off: she inspired in me a belief in faith, for which I'm grateful.

My mum was wise, protecting, and powerful. Every now and then, on a special occasion, she'd change out of her rubber gloves, no-iron-necessary everyday wear, into elegant, beautiful, handmade dresses, and come downstairs smelling of perfume, her face made up, her hair styled. We thought she looked incredibly glamorous, like women we saw on TV and in films. (We had little to compare her to except shop-keepers, teachers, and the women who served us dinner at school.)

With church on Sundays, confession every couple of weeks, and the occasional mass said at home by relatives who were priests, religion was an ongoing part of my childhood. Religious artifacts, some kitschy, others beautiful, speckled the house. My mum had just sent me one I found beautiful. I'd always thought it odd that Michelangelo's Mary looks as young as her son. It gives the statue sexual undertones. Maybe I read too much into it, but to me the crux of the matter is that her child is hurt and their love is deep. I can't imagine greater love than what a mother feels for her child. On the bottom of the statue was a sticker, exactly the kind of thing my mum would do; she might as well have colored it in with felt-tip pen like we kids did to the one I grew up with. I read my mum's writing.

Aiden. When I left you in Brussels, I asked Our Lady to put her arms around you and take care of you. She did that, so I thanked her when I went to Lourdes. When I saw this statue, it reminded me of when I left you and it seemed to me the only thing I could do for you was pray she would do a good job.

Love you, Mum

I stood beside my kitchen sink and cried. The kettle switched off; I made coffee. When I thought I was finished crying, I went into the living room and called David.

"Hey, bubby, I got a present from my mum."

"A present," said David, his voice like an excited child's. "What is it?"

"It's a statue. . . ."

I stopped talking. David knew instantly something was wrong.

"Baby, are you okay?"

I managed a squeaky "Yes."

"What is the statue of?"

"Michelangelo's *Pietà*."

My eyes flooded with tears. I still wasn't completely awake, and hadn't armored myself for the day. After a while, I was able to speak again.

"There's a sticker on the bottom—"

I broke into loud sobs. David waited patiently. Eventually, I read him the sticker.

After a moment, David said, "It must be lovely having a mother who cares so much."

"Believe me," I said. "It is. Sometimes she shocks me. I think her religion is silly, then she does this and shows how deep it is. She lives life concerning herself with shopping, nephews and nieces, everyday things, but she carries this depth of compassion I can only begin to imagine."

"You don't have to imagine it. You can feel it."

David and I continued talking for about ten minutes—I think just so he could be sure I was all right—then he said, "Actually, I'm in the middle of varnishing."

"Oh! I'm sorry."

"Don't worry."

"Do you like living there?" I asked.

"I miss you."

"That's a good answer. You're very slick."
"I'll see you at the gym. Love you."
"Not as much as my mum."
"More."
"You couldn't."
"You might be surprised."

30

Soon I was on a plane to New York, where Whatever had been booked to play three gigs. Once again Paul drove us to Heathrow, and once again Nina and I waited as he and Marc said their lingering good-bye. We wore our usual airplane costumes, but my hair was now blue-black, which no amount of mousse could conceal. I wore a cap, and in doing so probably looked more conspicuous.

After check-in, we ate an overpriced terminal breakfast, bought an unnecessary amount of chocolate for the flight, and boarded the plane. We were careful not to listen to the safety instructions, but watched the flight attendants anyway; they looked so funny, exact replicas of comic send-ups of the profession. I assume they registered this and got even by treating us like children. When we were bad (that is, had too much fun) or persisted in getting their attention, they punished us by being patronizing or, worse, ignoring us. If we were good (that is, bored and resigned), they behaved nicely and were more responsive (but only a little). Maybe I was being paranoid and they were just doing their jobs as usual. It's so hard to tell with cabin crew, since they nearly always act superior. I don't know whether this is because they think bopping around the world constantly touching up their hair and makeup is glamorous, or if their attitude is really resentment because the passengers—however dog-eared they become during the long hours onboard—actually get off at the end and do something interesting, whereas the crew have to turn around immediately and fly back (or do so immediately after sleeping over). Probably it's because, unlike real waiters, they don't have to work for tips and know that passengers are stuck with them—we can't escape—and therefore daren't piss them off even if they throw their prefab food at us. If this sounds like I've got a grudge, it's because I've had to put up with such flight crew misbehavior for years.

We killed time doing sitting-still-with-restricted-movement things. Eventually the captain informed us we were about to land, and in about half an hour more we actually did. After taxiing down the runway, the plane eased up to the boarding ramp and stopped. We stood, retrieved our hand luggage, and waited. This herding was the most excruciating part for Nina, Marc, and me; it was all we could do to stop ourselves from stampeding off the plane. We barely noticed our despised flight attendants doing their farewell-smile thing as we passed them, even though it was probably the closest thing to authentic feeling they'd shown since we'd boarded—it meant their job was almost done. (I imagine they breathed inward sighs of relief. I've heard cabin crew bitching about passengers; usually I'm just grateful it's not me they're talking about.)

The sun was setting at JFK. Marc had never been to New York City, so I asked the cabbie to take the most scenic route into Manhattan. As we drove, day turned to night. The sky changed color quickly: dusky red to brown to near-black. Skyscrapers sparkled with thousands of tiny lights.

Marc pressed his face against the window, staring out in awe. He wound down the window and breathed deeply, as if seeing wasn't enough; he wanted it in him, couldn't wait to be in it. He turned to me and smiled, bursting with his new experience. I should have felt happy for him, but envy was easier. Still, I managed to smile back.

After lots of lefts, rights, and traffic lights, we pulled off Madison Avenue onto East Seventy-third Street. It was the most we could do to acknowledge our hosts before we washed our faces, brushed our teeth, and crumpled into our beds, exhausted.

We woke predictably early and had breakfast in the diner across the street. Fed, and feeling more human, I asked Nina and Marc if they wanted to join me at the gym. I didn't feel like going myself, but thought I should: over the coming week a lot of people would be looking at me onstage. They opted to come with me, in part, I think, because they felt the same way I did, and because we were scheduled to have lunch with the organizer of one of our gigs, a man named Eric Conrad who ran Beige, a successful club night at the Bowery Bar in the East Village. Beige attracted New York's absolute-cool denizens, along with those who wanted to feel part of that crowd and somehow managed to get into the club. But first we had to get the gym out of the way. I chose David Barton on Sixth Avenue in Chelsea. It was the most familiar, and it was likely I'd see somebody I knew there.

I did—the extraordinary singer Joey Arias, who was by now an integral part of New York's infrastructure. As always, he was funny, shocking, and sleazy—altogether lovely. I also saw a rash of muscled men as familiar to me as the Manhattan skyline. I'd seen them for as long I'd been visiting New York. We knew things about each other, but had never bothered simply to get to know each other. A few months ago this sort of noninteraction would have plunged me into a tailspin. Not now; I enjoyed my workout despite it. Training was beginning to feel familiar again. I was regaining the body I'd had before, the body that other gym gays noticed—and, being noticed, I concluded that in this small world I counted once more. It wasn't that I hadn't learned anything from my recent brush with death, or that I wasn't cynical about such exchanges or credited them with having actual value. But I can't pretend I didn't like the attention now that it was once again coming my way.

Having showered and changed, Nina, Marc, and I headed to Bowery Bar feeling both rejuvenated and spent.

Baillie Walsh had introduced me to Eric, having talked him up no end—high praise coming from Baillie, who was himself so exceptional, a brilliant video director and filmmaker. But more important to me was his mixture of wisdom beyond his years, warmth, peerless yet accessible sense of humor, and his entertaining way of talking—creative, colloquial, sophisticated, yet very street. He was one of a very few people in my life I felt I never spent enough time with.

Eric therefore had a lot to live up to.

I soon saw what Baillie meant. Eric's mind was extremely active, his actions frenetic, his wit sharp—and prone to precision cutting. Over lunch at Bowery Bar, Nina, Marc, and I watched his brain forge ahead, only sometimes stopping to share his thoughts. In one breath he'd mention something about Beige and something about the gig he'd arranged for us at Limelight. Each new thought seemed to push out the preceding one, sometimes not giving either enough time to form completely (or at least for us to hear it). Eric was nice to us, but I don't know if this was because he liked us or because we were friends of Baillie's. Whichever it was, it had the same effect. We arranged to speak again, and returned to Seventy-third Street.

When we called Eric later that afternoon, he told us that Baillie had popped into town unexpectedly on his way to Los Angeles. He had to catch an early flight the next morning, and was staying at Rupert Everett and Rifat Ozbeck's place in Greenwich Village. Nina, Marc, and I headed downtown to join Baillie, Rifat, and Eric (Rupert was in Hollywood having a meeting about some film). I was fond of Rifat, whom I'd met many years ago through Baillie, in Amsterdam, before London was gay enough to have fun in. We spent the first part of the evening mostly talking about Whatever's upcoming gigs, with Rifat making suggestions as to what we should wear (he had designed the dress Nina wore for the Castro Street gig). Needless to say, we ended up getting wasted.

Dinner in the East Village had already been planned, and Nina, Marc, and I were invited along. There we met someone who was introduced as Chris Ciccone—Madonna's brother, we were told.

After dinner, all seven of us squeezed into a limousine and headed to Limelight to check out the stage. I'd been to the club many times before, but not for over five or six years. Limelight was located in a deconsecrated former Episcopal church on Sixth Avenue at Twentieth Street in Chelsea. We went in a back door, through a maze of tunnels, and ended up in the VIP bar, where I proceeded to get more wasted and the evening wound on until we found ourselves heading home, having completely forgotten to check out the stage. By then I'd spent a lot of time with Chris, as I'd ended up sitting next to him in the VIP bar. It turned out he had a paternal side, which was something I craved in my post-roadkill state of mind. When it came time to leave, he shared a cab with Nina, Marc, and me. I don't know if he lived uptown, or if anybody cared by then.

Somewhere in midtown, I asked where we were dropping Chris. Nina told him to come with us, which I thought polite and friendly. Once inside the apartment, however, suddenly Nina and Marc were nowhere to be seen—and I was left to host Chris. The strangest part was that we were in my bedroom. I really can't remember how this happened. Chris excused himself to use the bathroom. I took double my usual amount of sleeping tablets. I suppose that when Chris returned and found me asleep, he politely took his leave, because he was no longer there when I woke up.

31

The next day again began with breakfast across the street and the David Barton gym, but this time we had lunch at Manatus, a diner on Bleecker Street between Christopher and West Tenth Streets, in the heart of Greenwich Village. Manatus was always filled with gay men in their forties or older, some of whom seemed as though they might even be long-term couples. Watching them looking content, with warmth in their eyes, gave me hope that this might someday be possible for me. Of course, it could have been my imagination, and more likely they were woozy and grinning from an afternoon tipple. Whichever it was, some kind of happiness seemed to be present at Manatus, and I liked going there. After eating, we accompanied Marc to buy socks, and Nina to a health-food store to buy homeopathic remedies, then took a cab back uptown, ordered in Chinese, and went to bed, our internal clocks somewhat more aligned with the time zone.

Our first gig was on Monday, for the interiors magazine *Nest*, of which my friend—and our host—Joe Holtzman was the editor-in-chief and art director. It was a launch party for the Spring 1999 issue, and was to be held in a townhouse on Beekman Place that was featured in the issue. The talented and entirely adorable Todd Oldham had photographed the house together with Derry Moore. There was also an article about my apartment in London, which had been photographed by Johnnie Shand Kydd, somebody I'd modeled for many times and who had, I believed, an incredible ability to capture spontaneous moments as though he'd staged them for hours.

On arriving for our two o'clock sound check we realized that there was no stage—and therefore no stage lighting and no backstage area where we could prepare ourselves. A saving grace was our backdrop: a glass wall overlooking the East River. The house was the work of Paul Rudolph and was the most severe example of seventies interior design I'd ever seen: back-lit rectangular wall panels; lots of Lucite and Perspex; narrow, floating marble-and-steel staircases without railings; hard edges at every turn; black leather and beige carpet throughout. Transparent chairs and tables, a glass bathtub, a toilet that was part of a larger room, with no door for privacy and a sitting area immediately outside it—all added a voyeuristic element. It felt like a death trap. I wondered how the guests would navigate this brutal environment, and whether there would be any fatalities—especially once they had their guards lowered from drinking champagne.

Being a publishing event, the party was to start at six, which gave us little time to do anything else after finishing our sound check. At Joe's apartment we ate our pre-gig food and drank red wine, then got ready. Marc wore a white skirt and white see-through top, his hair tied close to the scalp in tiny pink loops: an androgynous mien to match his androgynous voice. Nina's brown chiffon evening dress from the 1950s complemented her skin color perfectly and made her black hair look more striking than ever. I wore a black suit I'd tied in knots, put in a washing machine, and tumble-dried, then untied, put on, and got Marc to sew to my body with elasticized thread. To finish off my retro-punk look, I spiked my hair with soap, applied a pale foundation to my face, and put blood-red lipstick over and around my eyelids (when I closed them, they looked like they'd been plucked). We did no coke before the gig, out of practicality rather than preference; we couldn't be bothered to organize getting it.

We could have walked from Seventy-third Street, but took a cab anyway. People milled around on the Beekman Place sidewalk, mostly "properly dressed" adults waiting to go inside. I felt like a freak, but understood that this was, in part, my job for the evening. I headed straight to a bar and drank about four glasses of champagne. Sid happened to be in New York and had come to the party; he assumed the role of our manager and introduced us to the packed audience. Nina, Marc, and I went to our microphones, pausing for a moment to marvel at the spectacular view, whose twinkling lights and muted colors of buildings along the East River made Whatever look subtle in comparison.

The audience was an unusual crowd, even for us. They nodded their heads in appreciation, clapped gloved hands, gently swung their bodies. Maybe we'd found our market niche. An old woman with drawn-on lips and thick foundation for skin tottered up to Marc and slowly pulled his hands to her forehead as though he were a holy man.

The last song of the evening, "Dead Boy," was the liveliest. I sang the first verse.

I kissed a boy who was dead
His lips were tinged with purple
His eyes gave no response
I took off my clothes
And I lay down

He was so cold that I felt cold beside him
He gave me nothing at all

Nina and Marc joined in for the chorus.

You can fuck me
Or lick me
Or hit me
And fiddle
It all means so little to me
You can choke me
Or poke me
Or fist me
And piddle
It all means so little to me
It all means so little to me

I sang the next verse alone.

I fucked a boy who was dead
And still there was no response
What is the purpose of this?
Without response
There's no joy
So when finished
He turned to me
And he said

All three of us sang the chorus—

You can fuck me
Or lick me
Or hit me
And fiddle

It all means so little to me
You can choke me
Or poke me
Or fist me
And piddle
It all means so little to me
It all means so little to me

—then Marc sang the middle eight solo.

My lips are tinged with purple and blue
They're bruised beyond belief
I have been lying here such a long time
That my skin is very cold
My eyes show no reaction at all
They do not want to hurt you
How can I give a response?
When all that you did was fuck me

To end on a high point, we put a great deal of energy into the last chorus, repeating it four times, each faster and more manic—

You can fuck me
Or lick me
Or hit me
And fiddle
It all means so little to me
You can choke me
Or poke me
Or fist me
And piddle
It all means so little to me
It all means so little to me

—ending with Marc singing the last line in a sweet, castrato-like octave:

IT ALL MEANS SO LITTLE TO ME

Then silence.

The audience began to clap—hesitantly, with none of the whistling or shrieking that often accompanied our performances. With no backstage to retreat to, we stepped gingerly into the crowd, who greeted us with politician-like handshakes and pats on shoulders. Full of post-gig adrenaline, we didn't mind. After a couple of hours chatting with party guests, we ended up hanging out with the fabulous Nadine Johnson, the head of a savvy New York public relations firm. Eventually we headed home for another early night (relatively speaking), worn out from being Whatever.

The following evening we had dinner at Food Bar on Eighth Avenue in Chelsea, where I introduced Nina and Marc to RonniLyn. I'd met Ronni-Lyn in 1997, when I was serving as guest editor of Sean Strub's *Poz* magazine. Sean had several cool, likable, and bright people working for him at the time, but RonniLyn was my favorite. Sean himself was all of the above, particularly good at making things happen—and, more importantly, seeing things through. I admired him, and found him an inspiration.

RonniLyn had brought along her friend Troy, who was visiting from Washington. After dinner, Nina went back to Ronnie's apartment for a joint. Marc, still not over his jet lag, felt "a bit AIDSy" and decided to return to Seventy-third Street. I went with Troy to Barracuda, a popular Chelsea gay bar, where we drank more (I was already drunk) and did cocaine; then we retired to Troy's place, had sex for hours, and fell asleep together.

Our Thursday gig at Limelight was pushed back by management to later than advertised, giving us two hours to kill. Troy joined us with cocaine; by the time we went onstage, Nina, Marc, and I were trashed. Nina wore only tights, her head through the gusset of a second pair. She looked nude, but somehow at the same time not nude. I was equally so, in a dress made from the same fabric. After much convincing, Marc wore his white outfit from Monday. The crowd was mostly bridge-and-tunnel teenage girls. Those in the front row looked both confused and wide-eyed, which changed as we went through our set. Every now and then I'd make eye contact with one of them and she'd smile shyly. I saw somebody I recognized—I wasn't sure how or from where—and nodded to him and raised my hand while I sang. He didn't respond. Later in the set, I moved to the other side of the stage and sat down at the edge, and saw him again. It was James, who'd worked on the film in San Fransisco. He smiled. I smiled back.

In the dressing room, we unwound by finishing Troy's cocaine, barely noticing the knocking on the door, then halfheartedly attempted to cover the drugs, even though we'd been told we could do whatever we wanted in the dressing room. It was James. I invited him in and introduced him to everybody. Before leaving he gave me his telephone number and asked me to call him. Once he was gone, Troy announced that he was jealous. I didn't respond.

We went upstairs to the after-show party in the VIP bar. I recognized lots of faces from the New York club scene, including a man I'd had a crush on years before. But our drugs didn't correspond, and we didn't talk long (he was on Ecstasy, sweaty and blissful, whereas I was dry and cynical, on coke). Others I refused to remember. After a couple of hours Troy told me he wasn't feeling well and asked me to take him home.

I hesitated. Part of me thought, *No way, I want to stay with my mates, have a laugh, and continue getting wasted.* Either this wasn't what I really wanted, or I was overwhelmed with a perverse sense of conscience, because I went and got Troy's and my coats, then found him puking on the stairs. Once home, he perked up enough to have sex. Needless to say, I was suspicious. The next day, we had brunch at Manatus and in the evening saw a film before returning to his place, where I lay holding him, feeling content and relaxed. He was restless.

"Do you fancy me?" he said at last.

"Yeah."

"You don't seem to want much sex."

"Compared to who?"

"I mean, for two guys who've just met."

"Do you think so?"

"Forgive me for being presumptuous, but . . ."

He stopped. I must have looked apprehensive, virtually wincing as I guessed the end of his sentence. When people use this phrase, I can't help thinking they don't really mean *forgive me*, but rather *I feel completely justified in what I'm about to say.*

"What?" I said, already resigned.

"Well, considering who you are, what you're famous for. On the videos . . ."

He paused again. I seized the opportunity.

"That's not real."

"I know that."

I got out of bed. "You know that what you're saying is kind of creepy."

"Where are you going?"

"Firstly, to the bathroom, but then anywhere I can be by myself."

I pissed, unable to believe what I'd just heard. When I returned and he didn't say anything to repair the situation, I started getting dressed.

"Is this what you want?"

"No."

"What do you want, some oily, overtanned, two-dimensional freak who talks porn-speak?"

"No."

"Can't I just be RonniLyn's friend, the guy you met in Food Bar?"

"Yeah. I'm sorry."

I didn't believe he was sorry. Confused, maybe. What seemed clear was that his version of me was a fantasy. It was freezing outside and he was a warm body, so I spent the night. As soon as I woke, I escaped.

32

Allowing myself a day to recover, I went to the gym. Neither Nina nor Marc wanted to come with me, so I knew it would be nearly unbearable. It was hideous. Thanks to coke my tolerance threshold and paranoia were ripe. I'm a tough enough cookie, though—I could behave as ignorantly and rudely as the worst of them—and I got through it, even managing to smile and thank the weird (but I guessed he thought he was great-looking) man on the desk, who looked at me as though I hadn't just communicated. (Maybe he was intuitive and knew what I was thinking, or maybe he was thinking about his laundry. I made a mental note not to be so transparent, just in case.) That evening I ordered in Chinese food and stared at the TV with Marc (Nina had gone out with Ronnilyn). Before bed, we took several Valiums.

I woke the next morning feeling barely rested. My body clock was warped. I lay in bed hoping to revive; before long I opened my eyes, if only to let visually instigated thoughts replace the involuted negativity I experienced with them closed. I watched the lemon-gray sky outside the window slowly turn turquoise, then blue. New York was waking; people were starting their days. I felt envious, voyeuristic, lonely. Eventually my feelings focused on sadness, then anxiety. I gave in and got up, distracting myself with breakfast. It was so primitive: I felt hunger and satisfied it; eating, like having sex, allowed me to feel in control of my life.

Waking early meant I had a whole day to wait before our gig at Jackie Sixty, where we were to perform on a queer/punk night called Mother hosted by Chi Chi Valenti and Johnny Dynell. Sound check wasn't until eight, and Whatever didn't go on until one-thirty in the morning. Thanks to my accident, I'd had a great deal of practice waiting for days to end. I killed time (an appropriate expression) doing laundry, making phone calls, dragging myself around. Nina and Marc were keen to visit the Central Park Zoo, probably because I had talked it up. I loved the setting—a bit of wilderness, however tamed, with skyscrapers peeping over the trees—although I found it sad seeing the caged animals. I loved losing myself watching the polar bears, their perfect grace as they darted around, diving and splashing in and under the water (which you could see through a glass wall). It should have been even more rewarding doing it with two of my best friends, but neither they nor the bears affected me. I felt jaded, and hoped it was due to the drugs I was taking. (It was easier to blame my self-indulgent feelings on trauma brought on by my accident.)

Thinking ahead, none of us wanted to come all the way back uptown after the sound check. Jackie Sixty was in the meatpacking district of Greenwich Village, a couple of blocks from the Hudson River. I remembered that James lived on Christopher Street, and called him to explain our predicament. He invited us to hang out and get ready at his place, although I heard uncertainty in his voice. I called Troy, just to keep him updated, and told him our plan. He was furious.

"What's wrong?" I said, surprised.

"I know how you two met."

"That's because I told you."

"Do you expect me not to be annoyed?"

"It would be nice."

"You've had sex with him."

"I've had sex with thousands of men."

"Do you expect me not to be jealous?"

"I've no idea what I expect, if anything."

"Can I come with you?"

"There's already three of us, and he didn't sound too sure about *us* on the phone."

"You're impossible."

"Help me out. We don't want to trek uptown. I don't suppose we could come to your place."

"It's not my place."

"James's it is, then."

"Do whatever you want. I'll be fine."

"Please, it will be so much easier for us."

"You two better not be together at the club."

"I'll be with you."

"Okay, but understand that I'm jealous."

I tried, but couldn't.

"I'll probably see you at the club then," he said.

"What do you mean, *probably*?"

"I mean I'll see you at the club."

"I'll leave your name at the door."

I was exhausted and riled. I concentrated on my breathing. No matter how much I tried to relax, my exhales and inhales wavered. I got up, took two painkillers, and impatiently stuffed a toothbrush and a change of clothes in my bag, then watched a talk show host screw up somebody's life. As the TV credits rolled, Nina walked into my room wearing her coat. It was finally time to leave for the sound check.

Sid turned up late. I didn't mind. As a rule I tried not to notice him. I couldn't help seeing the sleep in the corners of his eyes, the constant puzzled look on his face. He wore suits without shirts. He wore hats—bowlers, trilbies, any style with character—to cover up his thinning hair. All of this to make up for a personality like a caricature of somebody with character. Sid was a wheeler-dealer, a ducker and a diver, traits we overlooked, thinking they might come in handy when talking to record companies.

Sound check went smoothly, mainly because the soundman did a great job. We left feeling optimistic, and went around the corner to Café Florent to grab something to eat. The diner was packed with a trendy, after-work crowd. We didn't fit in at all—which may be why, despite repeatedly raising our hands for attention, we managed only to get stared at and ignored. Eventually we gave up and left. Sid went back to where he was staying, mumbling something about keys, cats, and meeting us later at the club. We picked up a bottle of vodka and headed for Christopher Street.

James's apartment was cozy and he was hospitable; it felt like a good decision to have gone there. Half a glass of vodka and cranberry later, I began to relax. It was natural hanging out with James; although I didn't know him well, he felt like an old friend. Since he was a visual artist, I suggested that he draw something on Marc for the performance. They both agreed. James did a jigsaw-puzzle design on Marc's arms, and at my instigation wrote a list of words on his back. I'd call out words—*shit*, *fuck*, *baby*, *dogs*—and down they went, like a spine. Nina decided to wear her stocking outfit again, and wanted some writing that would show through the fabric. James wrote WHATEVER across her chest in large capital letters with a sprinkling of black dots. I wore my dress from the Limelight gig, and had James wrap clear packaging tape around my arms, making them look disfigured—a recurring theme of mine. I wanted people to like me, but went to great lengths to repel them. My reasoning: I wanted them to like me for everything *I might be*—no matter how ugly, effeminate, stupid, ridiculous, or obtuse.

I mentioned to James that I was tired, whereupon he got up, went to the kitchen, rummaged in a draw, and returned with some crystal. Two lines later, I felt more awake, ready to face an audience. (Like many performers, even some quite famous ones, I felt anxiety about nearly every gig. The whole day before and after revolved around preparing and recovering, which made me wonder if I was cut out for such a gregarious profession. Part of me wanted to retire beside a lake, to walk into town for supplies, to not act like a freak and be gawked at onstage. It must have fulfilled some need in me, though, having to do, perhaps, with ego, acceptance, plain old showing off, and, very likely, sex.)

We did more crystal, with vodka chasers, then went to the club and immediately headed to our dressing room to collect ourselves. James stayed with us, fetching drinks from the bar, chopping lines, and generally being useful. At one point, I thanked him for his help, planting a noisy, childlike kiss on his forehead.

Immediately a loud, indignant sigh sounded from the dressing room doorway. I turned. There stood Troy, clearly pissed off.

"Hey baby!" I said.

"What are you doing?" he demanded.

"I was just saying thanks to James."

"Is that how you say thanks?"

"Sometimes."

"It looked more like making out."

"It wasn't a real kiss."

"It looked like a real kiss."

Troy got angrier as he spoke. He snatched the beer bottle I had in my hand; for a moment, I thought he was going to hit me with it.

Nina stepped between us, saying, "No. No. No. Not before we go on, please." Gently but firmly she ushered Troy out of the room; when she'd shut the door behind him, she smiled and said, "Shoo!"

Five minutes later came a knock. We looked at each other, exasperated. A small voice followed.

"Hey guys, it's Sid. Let me in."

Nina opened the door as we greeted Sid with laughter.

"They want you on. I said I was heading down here and I'd let you know."

During our set the crowd looked like they were listening, which we enjoyed. Some even danced. It was a great gig, for us at least (and after all, that was what it was really about). Afterward we snuck downstairs to our dressing room to drink and talk about the set. Troy turned up and began giving me grief again. I tried to explain that it wasn't a good time. I was full of adrenaline, in no mood to be serious about something I cared nothing about.

Marc's response was to lower his head and keep quiet. Nina, as usual, came to my rescue.

"Aiden," she said, "do you want Troy here?"

I hesitated. He was pushing me to the limits of my patience.

"Would you rather deal with this tomorrow?" Nina reworded her question.

"Yes," I said.

Nina took Troy by the arm again, speaking to him in a soothing voice.

"But Aiden," he said, standing in the doorway, tears in his eyes, "you can't . . ."

"Yes, he can," said Nina. "He needs time to himself. Please."

She pushed Troy out the door, locking it this time, then dusted off her hands as if she'd just thrown out the garbage.

"Thank God!" said Marc. "He was killing me. I don't know how you put up with him, Aiden."

"He's only a baby."

"They're always babies," said Nina. "That's the problem."

"Ron was the same age as me," I said.

"I know you're saying something about age," said Marc, "but all I'm hearing is, *sex sex sex sex sex sex sex*."

"Enough!"

James joined in. "I couldn't believe you went for that kid in your last video."

"Luke had his good points."

"Like what?" said Marc. "Being there when you needed him?"

"You should all join Troy, you'd probably get on great."

"All I'm saying is, you could try somebody more your own age," said James. He smiled. Then, realizing what he'd said, he put his head down, embarrassed.

We did crystal and drank beer until Jackie Sixty closed. Nina and Marc wanted to continue at an after-hours joint. James, who had an irregular heartbeat, felt an episode coming on and needed to get home. He asked if I'd like to join him. Troy was long gone, and the alternative was sitting in some dingy bar or trolling a sex club or sauna, so I said yes; familiarity often won out over adventure (or whatever it was I'd so often done for so many years). Nina and Marc left with Sid, and I jumped into a cab with James.

The next thing I remember is Marc calling from a pay phone. It was daylight outside. Nina and Sid had abandoned Marc, and he had no money to get home. I told him to cab over to James's.

The apartment was a mess of drug and sex debris. Marc laughed a little about this, but seemed on his last bit of energy. We talked for a while, toying with the idea that Nina might be having sex with Sid as we spoke, then agreed that it seemed unlikely. I called Manatus and ordered breakfast for Marc. Being more dressed than James and me, Marc answered the door when the food arrived.

The deliveryman was far too large for his uniform, which made him look good enough to eat. He smiled the biggest, dumbest, most beautiful John Travolta smile and said, "Sorry about your wait."

Completely exhausted, Marc somehow summoned the energy to say, "What's wrong with my weight? Am I too fat or too thin?"

The man got the joke and laughed, saying, "Don't worry, you're good."

This took Marc off guard.

"I know you're just being sweet, but at this time of the morning it's just what the doctor ordered. Thank you."

This interaction was enough to heal the wounds Marc's ego had sustained during his evening out in Manhattan. By the time he headed uptown, he was in better shape mentally and physically than when he'd arrived at James's.

James and I took sleeping tablets. We woke later in the day, ate breakfast at six P.M., and went back to bed. In the morning, James complained that I'd taken up too much of the bed. I remembered waking up, maneuvering into the middle, putting James's arm around me, and holding on to it. I explained my fear of falling out of bed. He barely listened. I found it difficult to get people to understand. I guess it was hard to believe that, only months before, I'd been paralyzed and in a wheelchair. I found it exhausting and upsetting explaining, and usually didn't bother.

I'd slept through Sunday, and spent Monday preparing to fly back to London. We had to rise at five to get to the airport on time. By now my body clock was so confused, it hardly mattered that it was so early. About an hour after takeoff, I started to cry. I cried every hour or so after that. I couldn't stop for long. I ate my supper and breakfast crying. At some point, a flight attendant laid a box of tissues on my tray as she passed, without stopping or drawing attention to me. I thought this kind and respectful of her; it showed the best side of how the British could be.

The sky, black when we took off, gained color as we headed into morning. I leaned against the window, my face ghostly against the outside and reflected cabin, continuing to cry as I watched the sun rise. When the captain announced we were about to land, I stopped abruptly. A flight attendant (I presumed it was the same one) came and crouched beside me, placing one hand on my armrest, the other over one of mine.

"This is meant to be for me," she said, giving me a big box of chocolates, "but I'd like you to have them."

Paul picked us up at Heathrow. Seeing him and Marc being affectionate made me writhe. Paul even had a homecoming present for me. All I could feel was resentment. When they dropped me off at my front door, I asked Marc to walk me inside.

The flat was bleak and freezing. I checked the thermostat; the heating was broken. Marc hugged me, saying he'd call me later. I closed the door behind him and started to cry again—quietly, so Marc wouldn't hear. I went to my kitchen cupboard, took down an old box of antidepressants, and popped two from their blister packet. My sad feelings were probably due to the aftereffects of crystal, but I told myself I'd gone off antidepressants too soon. I always found some justification when it came to taking drugs. As I placed the tablets in my mouth, it struck me that they had become a crutch, and I wondered if perhaps I was just swapping old addictions for a new, albeit state-of-the-art, legal, socially acceptable one. At least it was pharmaceutical grade, I reassured myself.

I'd passed the chocolates on to Nina, to give to her boyfriend, Russell. They were too unhealthy for David, and by then Marc was sick of chocolate, having consumed so much during the flight.

33

Even on antidepressants, if I wasn't constantly distracted I'd drop into a less happy layer of myself and stare into space. I experimented with raising the dose to twice a day. It worked, but there was a drawback: I lost my urge to have sex, and with it what I believed to be an essential part of my personality. Put simply, like the taste of sugar or salt or fat, the smell of burning wood in the night air, or the feeling of a spring morning, cumming made my life more worth living.

Things settled, but too much. Everything seemed flat—without anxiety and torment, yes, but also without compassion and desire. I wanted *some* fluctuation of mood, just not an overwhelming amount. I cut back to one antidepressant a day. A slight sex drive returned. After about a week, I had a celebratory wank. With imagination, focus, and patience, eventually I came. I felt functioning, alive, normal.

Christmas reared its ugly head. I expected the worst and it didn't let me down. All I could see was cold-looking daylight outside my living room window. Where was the festive TV Christmas, the carols, the goddamn pop-song version? Surely it came to an affluent area like Chelsea. Apparently not. I felt only vague bleakness. Was I truly jaded, finally, or merely resigned to not being more family-oriented, more popular, more whatever it was I couldn't attain, no matter how much money I spent on trying to make the fantasy real? More likely, the antidepressants I was taking had something to do with it. Maybe I hadn't read the contraindications in the box properly, and they clearly stated that the pills could delay ejaculation and negate the holiday spirit.

I was on the verge of canceling Christmas with sleeping tablets when Marc called, all cheerful, insisting that I join him at Paul's for dinner. I put away the tablets and went to endure the spectacle of their being in love. (How much reminding did I need that I didn't have a boyfriend?) They cooked a sickeningly delicious dinner, and I tried to drink away my gloom. I called David, knowing he'd been working hard all day and might be up for some fun, and he came round in his car to rescue me from the excruciating domestic bliss at Paul's.

He took me to More, where I spent time standing around. Usually when out in a club, I'd be surprised how quickly I'd get lost in the noise, sex, sweat, and drugs. Now I was aware of what time it was. Even though I'd taken as many stimulants as anybody there, I couldn't get into the mood of things. Maybe I just wasn't on the right drug cocktail. Thankfully, David soon said he was over it and wanted to go home. I told him I was over it too, but about five years previous. I collected a boy and we left.

Six days later, I spoke to David in the evening, as he was planning an early night. He wasn't one to make a fuss about things like New Year's Eve. On one hand I admired him for never getting swept up in such nonsense; on the other—and it's my only criticism of him—he lacked a sense of occasion. I spent the night watching celebrations on TV. A lot of people might think this sad, but after such a hectic year it felt right to be quiet and still, safe in my home.

The outside world returned to normal. People were back at work. Trains and buses ran at their usual times. Mail was once again being delivered. I woke to find a frequent-flyer statement among mine. I'd accumulated over fifty thousand miles, enough for a transatlantic flight, and I was ready to lie in the sun, splash in the sea, and miss sleep because the nights were too warm for comfort. I called Guido in South Beach and asked if I could stay with him.

The first available flight to Florida was three weeks away, which felt like a jail sentence. When the day finally arrived, the flight felt even longer. Guido picked me up at the airport. The ride to his house reminded me how reckless he was. It didn't seem fair to ask him to slow down or drive carefully, so I reminded myself how Marc or David would deal with the situation. David would say, "Live for the moment, enjoy the thrill." Marc would say, "Look on the bright side: You might crash." I opted for something in between. Taking a deep breath, I turned to the Miami skyline, noting the lavender lighting under the bridge across the harbor, the skyscraper lit with different colors throughout the year that was now white, and the patchy strip lighting from another causeway. I imagined these were my last moments on earth. Not believing in an after-life, I had no God to say anything to, no apologies to make, no preparing to do. It occurred to me that the experience might be more sensational with scented night air rushing past my face. Briefly acknowledging that the window going down might distract Guido and actually cause an accident, I took another deep breath and pressed the button to open the window.

My trip to South Beach was unremarkable. I stood on the shore watching the sea undulate, the clouds float, the sun set. Eyes closed, I listened to crashing waves, squawking gulls, the murmur of music from bars along Ocean Drive. I expected to feel something, if only an appreciation of nature, but I didn't. I thought to lose myself in drugs at a nightclub and thereby forget that I wasn't ready for such a focus on the physical, but I didn't. Hard as I tried to get something out of being there, South Beach gave nothing back. After seven days, I returned early to London.

I slept in quite late. I spent so much time traveling, only to be grateful to come home. Maybe this was why I did it. My flat, my bed, my pillow, sheets, duvet—I loved them. I hadn't been away long enough for my body clock to go much out of sync, but it had been long enough, as Marc told me seconds after my first coffee, for Nina to be seeing—to be in love with—Sid. She'd asked her old boyfriend to move out of her apartment. Marc and I were surprised. Russell was sweet, clever, and beautiful. Sid wasn't particularly brilliant, and used his version of charm to make up for this. To Marc and me, it came across as smarmy, a quality we thought useful in a manager but not in the lover of one of our best mates.

I went to the gym and did a grueling workout, telling myself as I exercised how lucky I was that my body did what I wanted it to. Afterward, I went to Notre Dame de France, a church off Leicester Square, and lit candles for people I loved. It looked like a service was about to commence; I knelt to listen. A group of nuns sang Vespers. Their voices penetrated me, reminding me of a time when being in church meant something to me. By going there now, I was hoping to feel a heightened sense of solitude. I wasn't disappointed, but I wasn't moved either. I took in what Hollywood refers to as a feel-good movie. I laughed once, smiled twice, and left the theater feeling no better than before I'd entered.

It was dusk. I walked through the crowds in Piccadilly Circus, down toward the Mall. I entered St. James's Park and headed to the pond, where I sat on a bench. I liked parks empty of people. Ducks and geese hissed and quacked, distracting me until, feeling self-conscious, I moved on (I always felt suspect being in a park after dark). I headed in the direction of Buckingham Palace, crossed into Green Park, and was struck by the smell of soil. Apart from the occasional jogger, this park also was empty. Things sharpened as the sun set. The cloudy sky produced pink-amber light that reflected off the white stitching on my trainers and clusters of snowdrops. I heard muffled squeals of children beyond the underpass to Hyde Park. I headed for the rose garden.

Someone came up beside me, glanced briefly over, looked away, then back at me. I smiled. He moved ahead of me.

"Hi," I said.

"Hello." He continued onward, an arm's length in front of me.

"Have you just come from work?"

"The suit's a bit of a giveaway, hey?"

"Do you work near here?"

"Park Lane."

"In one of the hotels?"

"No."

Silence. He maintained his pace.

"Do you like it here?" I said.

"Yeah. Bloody police, though. They've been here nearly every day lately."

"At least we're probably safe."

"Listen, I'm turning back. There's police ahead."

"So what? It's not as though we're cruising."

No answer. Maybe I wasn't supposed to use the "c" word. Finally, the man said, "Be careful."

"Okay, Captain," I said, saluting as he left.

There were no police ahead, just a man on a bicycle. Once out of the rose garden, the park was completely empty.

The sun had set. All was quiet. I stopped walking and looked around me.

It was a beautiful evening, the air surprisingly warm. I spotted a bank of snowdrops next to a weeping willow tree, the perfect place to rest. I lay back, head on the ground, grass tickling my ears, imagining I was cat, rabbit, hedgehog height, then closed my eyes in an attempt to focus and not be distracted by the sights around me.

The ground smelled stronger than ever.

Sounds of traffic, muted—the hum of car engines at the outskirts of the park.

Ducks quacking in the distance.

A strong, sweet smell I didn't recognize.

I opened my eyes and turned my head, trying to follow the scent, hoping to see where it came from: several bushes and, quite close behind them, a circle of street lamps. (This surprised me; I'd thought I was farther away, more alone.) Although the sky was thick with clouds, the odd star peeped through. To my left was the expanse of the Serpentine, and a bridge on which cars lined up bumper-to-bumper, their headlights and taillights throwing long slits of white and red onto the surface of the water.

I watched the lake. The ripples. The colors. The patterns.

Something stirred in me. I realized with surprise that I wanted to be happier—and that it might be possible.

But I needed help, and suddenly it was obvious where to get it.

I got up, brushed off the seat of my jeans, and headed toward the distant lights on the bridge.

Part Four
Ready to Begin Again

34

It took me hours of searching before I found what I was looking for in the old address book I'd kept for just such an occasion. Enthusiastically, I dialed. A man answered and said I must have the wrong number, sounding put out. Disappointed, I scoured my memory until I was finally able to dredge up her second name, and called directory assistance, which gave me a number in the area where I used to see her. I became hopeful— and anxious. I called David. He encouraged me to make the call as soon as I hung up with him. I promised that I would.

I put the phone down . . . and decided to make coffee, to help me clear my head so I'd be better able to express myself when I did call. Then the washing machine needed emptying, the rubbish needed putting out, vitamins needed to be taken. Eventually I ran out of chores, and only then did I admit that I was finding things to avoid doing what I knew I had to do.

I willed myself to the phone, sat down, and dialed. It rang. Someone picked up. I recognized her voice.

Gaia.

I'd seen Gaia for years in my twenties, when I was taking drugs at least four days a week and on the other three was so drunk I didn't notice the comedown. My relationship with my family, especially my mum, was almost nonexistent, and my relationships with men often consisted of degrading or abusive sex with no emotional attachment. I had just discovered I was HIV-positive, and because the use of protease inhibitors hadn't yet been developed, I was expecting to die soon of AIDS. And to say I was angry about this would be an understatement. Gaia helped me to handle these things. I couldn't think why I'd stopped seeing her.

Gaia sounded pleased to hear from me. She asked how I was. I told her, sticking mainly to the highlights: doing the movie, falling in love, getting hit by the car, being paralyzed. A couple of times she said, "Oh, dear." When I finished, we were both quiet for a moment. Then, "Are you all right?" she said, tenderness and concern in her voice.

"Nothing a bit of therapy wouldn't fix," I said.

She laughed.

"Can I see you? Do I qualify?"

"It would be lovely to see you."

"I think I need help. Don't you?"

"Let's talk, and then we can decide if we should meet regularly."

We made an appointment.

When I put down the receiver, I knew I'd just done something important for myself. I also knew that I had a long way to go.

During our meeting, I attempted to tell Gaia everything that had happened from the time I met Luke. It had been years since I'd last seen her, but the recent past seemed particularly significant. For an hour and a half I talked quickly, almost without pausing, apart from when I cried. At the end of the session, Gaia offered to see me for two hours once a week.

"But, before we go any further," she said, pausing to count on her fingers. "Yes. In a year's time next month, I'll be ending my practice."

"I'll have to talk twice as fast then," I said lightly.

She smiled—Gaia always responded to my jokes, no matter how weak they were—then said, "Try and remember that, won't you?"

35

Ran telephoned Marc from Brussels. He was hosting a new club and wanted Whatever to play. He offered us plenty of money as incentive, perhaps in the hope of mending, or at least making up for, our last trip and the accident, determined that the concert should actually take place this time. We agreed to Ran's terms. Although Sid had nothing to do with our being hired, he demanded twenty percent of Whatever's fee. Marc and I said that ten percent seemed fairer for a manager, but we didn't care enough to argue and Nina wouldn't get involved because she didn't want to take sides.

Regardless of whether or not Sid was indeed our manager, Nina and Marc seemed more apprehensive for my sake than I was. Gaia thought we should address the accident to prepare me for the trip, and during our sessions before Whatever left for Brussels it was our main topic. Without fail I cried, but still I couldn't remember anything about the accident and its immediate aftermath, only from when I woke up in Chelsea and West-minster Hospital. I'd begun to wonder how much of this memory was real and how much I'd pieced together from what Marc and David had told me. I asked Gaia if being in Brussels would make me remember more. She said she didn't know. I liked her response. When people had definitive answers to questions regarding the mind, it tended to make me suspicious.

Whatever recorded new tracks especially for the gig, and fine-tuned the ones we already had. During rehearsal, Nina kept saying how in love she was with Sid, acting as though she were glowing. To Marc and me she just seemed manic. She professed to feeling virginal. It was too easy to joke, and we tried not to. I may not have liked how Nina was behaving, and I certainly thought she was too good for Sid, but I wanted to support her as best I could, even though I saw a woman I loved fading daily.

The Brussels trip was only for a weekend. We were picked up at the airport, lodged at an expensive hotel, taken for fancy meals, and generally treated incredibly well. Sid tagged along with us—unnecessary, but Nina was enthusiastic. We didn't see much of her once we got to the hotel. Things had changed. Doing a gig away from London used to feel special, mainly because Marc, Nina, and I were together and Whatever was about friendship. Now it was about Nina and Sid having romantic getaways, and Marc and me trying not to care. Nina falling in love with Sid reminded me of when I'd fallen for Luke. Like me, I think Nina badly wanted to experience being in love, and (also like me) it didn't matter how bad a friend it made her. Increasingly I felt that part of the reason I'd been with Luke was that I was unconsciously determined to prove that prostitution hadn't fucked with my head too much to have a lover. Deep down, I think both Nina and I felt we'd been acutely hurt by our sex work, although we told ourselves that we were simply making the most of what we had while we still had it, whether it was using our youth and good looks in our twenties or salvaging what was left of them now. In the same way that I wasn't happy during a lot of my relationship with Luke, I didn't believe Nina was really happy with Sid. Her face too often seemed rigid, with a smile like that of an antique porcelain doll, the kind of smile that made you want to smash the doll into pieces.

Clearly it's unfair of me to project myself onto Nina, and perhaps my seeing Gaia again had made me prone to cheap psychologizing with my friend, but Nina and I had often found ourselves to be very much alike. As an adult, I felt I should be able to talk to her about the situation with Sid, but somehow this seemed impossible. Maybe I wasn't a good enough friend. If I told Nina what I really felt, it could cause a rift between us, which was the last thing I wanted. If I kept quiet, it seemed almost certain we'd drift apart anyway. Some might say I was jealous of Sid because he'd taken such a huge part of somebody I loved, but surely this would have been worth talking to Nina about, too.

With such thoughts on my mind, I barely managed to be natural around Nina, and in a way was relieved when she spent all her time with Sid. On Sunday, our last night in Brussels, all of us had dinner with Ran and other people connected with the club. I sat next to Nina, glad of the opportunity to be close, and asked her about her day. She told me that as she'd walked along the street earlier she'd looked down at the cracks in the pavement, which reminded her of when she used to walk to the hospital during our last trip, to visit me, which had been difficult because her own injured leg made walking very painful. As she spoke, her voice changed pitch. The rest of the table continued eating dinner, oblivious. Nina said it was my fault she was hit by the car, and kept going in that vein, gathering momentum. She stopped only when Marc intervened. He couldn't hear us from where he was, but noticed the dynamic of our interaction. (I was crying, more from seeing my friend so upset than anything else.) To distract Nina, Marc showed her the new nail varnish he'd bought that day, then glanced at me with a concerned smile.

We were paid in Belgian francs, which we exchanged for pounds in the airport on our return to England. Sid waited for his cut, watching the money being counted. Marc and I grudgingly paid him his twenty percent. On the phone later that night, Marc remarked that the next time we did a gig abroad he was going to bring Paul and that I should bring a date—and we should pay them both twenty percent of Whatever's fee.

Despite all this, it felt to me like a fairly successful trip. The audience seemed confused by Whatever, but we were used to this and half expected it by now. Sundays in London, a woman often stands on the street corner outside my apartment very early in the morning, singing songs about God through a megaphone. Some have melodies I recognize, some don't; sometimes I think she makes them up as she sings. This is kind of how I saw Whatever onstage, the only differences being that my Sunday-morning woman had but one subject and Whatever made a little more effort with how we looked. And it was as likely we'd get a record deal as she would.

36

Thank God I had Gaia to air my thoughts with. I'd hate to have done it to David—not that I hadn't for years already—but it was probably more useful to do it to somebody trained to deal with it, who could help make it better in some way.

Whatever had done surprisingly few drugs in Brussels, and it only took a couple of days before I felt fit for the gym. Working out has been one of the most consistent things in my life since I was about nineteen, comparable to eating, shitting, sleeping, my family, and Marc. All were irregular, but always present to some degree.

One afternoon, getting changed in the locker room, I was talking to a man named Seth. He looked like a bewildered raccoon, his uncropped hair shaggy with a fringe, under which he wore the kind of glasses meant to make you look clever. His skin was neither suntanned nor waxed; his clothes looked as though he was aware of fashion, but in a remote and strange small town. I was drawn to him partly because he was in front of me and partly because he seemed interested, but mostly because I was lonely.

The next time I saw him we were finishing our workouts at the same time. We talked until we'd changed, then discovered we were headed for the same tube stop. He said he was going to grab a coffee and asked me to join him, and within minutes he told me he was in a relationship of seven years' standing. I relaxed, assuming he was just being friendly and probably not looking for sex. When we finished our coffee, I said I'd enjoyed talking to him. I assumed I wouldn't see him again for a while.

I was wrong. He was at the gym the following day. I thought it odd I hadn't noticed him before, and told him so. He explained that he'd formerly worked out later, and had decided to start coming in the morning. This seemed reasonable. We again finished at the same time and over coffee he told me he was a writer who freelanced as an editor and considered himself an academic, with three degrees to prove this. (How many did it take?) After our conversation, the only thing I was sure about was how Seth identified himself. This left me wondering if I also created a model of what I was. If so, it couldn't be anything I was brought up to think admirable, good, or right.

Seth and I began hanging out together. He kept his own hours and he was often free. (His boyfriend worked late in the city.) We'd spend time doing nothing in particular—the odd workout, lunch, occasionally a film. Marc was still with Paul, Nina with Sid. David, hoping for a career in computers, was attending one course after another. Which left me alone, in need of distraction to keep me from getting depressed. Seth was a good distraction. He was bright and, like most editors I knew, held a vast amount of information from having read so much. His knowledge was "a mile wide and an inch deep," he said. I thought this cute until I realized he had an expression for everything, which quickly got annoying. When I asked him why he did it, he told me language was incredibly rich and he liked to have fun with it. I kept quiet, thinking if language was so rich, why cheapen it with catchphrases?

One afternoon, Seth asked if he could see my flat. Shortly after we got there, he asked could he lie down, saying that he didn't feel well. I felt sorry for him, and sat at the foot of the bed to keep him company. After a couple of minutes, he took hold of my arm, pulled me down, and kind of wrapped himself in me. I found this childlike and cute. Then Seth pushed his ass against my crotch. Surprised, I said nothing. He pressed back more, like a dog in heat. Despite this unflattering picture in my head, my cock began to stiffen. Instantly Seth flipped over, his face now a centimeter from mine, his hot breath on my lips, his hand sliding inside the front of my jeans. It felt gorgeous. He kissed me. This felt even better. Consumed with an uncharacteristic attack of conscience, I pulled back.

"Do you think this is a good idea?"

"It feels good."

"Good isn't the same as it being right."

"Trust me, I know what I'm doing."

Seth broke up with his boyfriend and asked if he could stay with me. I said yes, and got to know him better. In public he acted nice, and people generally took to him. He'd been brought up to be polite. He called old ladies "ma'am" and male cabdrivers "sir." Alone with me, he revealed a darker streak. The more I got to know Seth, the weirder he became. He was extremely possessive and jealous, accusing me of having sex with somebody if I washed the sheets while he was out. He said spiteful things he knew would wound me. He was exhausting, neurotic, even more self-obsessed than I was, and I think kookier, too. Sadly, I didn't feel in a position to turn down an opportunity not to be lonely. "Any port in a storm," was my excuse. It didn't take much on my side; all I had to do was exist.

My close friends were shrewd enough to notice something was wrong. Marc was the first to say something. When I asked what he thought of

Seth, he shuddered. "Ugh!" Pushed, he said Seth gave him the creeps, that he didn't trust him. Nina said, "I don't think Seth really likes women. I mean, any women, in any way." David simply wasn't around much; I should have read his absence as a sign.

Seth's ex-boyfriend called day and night, being rude and threatening me. I told Seth I was going to change my number. Gaia advised me to let him call, if I could bear it, that he needed to vent his frustration. I did as she suggested until it wore me out, then I asked Seth if he had anyone else with whom he could stay. By now we were married, in his mind at least, and my asking him to leave mortified him. Perhaps he'd had the safety of a relationship for so long, he'd forgotten there are basic rules if you want someone to want to be around you—like you're meant to be nice at least some of the time.

I may have appeared patient with Seth, even compliant. Maybe I was. Possibly it seemed that I'd engineered the whole episode, from the initial changing-room chitchat to him ditching his long-term boyfriend to him being crazy with jealousy. I hope not. But if I did, why? I got little out of it apart from Seth's company, decidedly a mixed bag. Was I that desperate for distraction?

Escape from Seth came in the form of an invitation for Whatever to play two gigs in the States. It would mean my missing a couple of therapy sessions, but I thought getting away from Seth would be more beneficial. For a few days he threatened to go with us, then backed out. I asked why. He said he'd hate to see me getting attention from so many men.

"That must be hard for him," Gaia observed when I told her, then added, "It would for a lot of people." Like David, I sometimes found Gaia too forgiving and generous about those giving me trouble. What I wanted to hear was, "He's bad. Keep away from him." If only life were that simple. Still, Gaia helped me deal with Seth. (Maybe too well; if I hadn't been seeing Gaia, I might not have been able to do more than say hello to Seth at the gym.)

Sid assumed he was accompanying Whatever on our mini-tour to San Francisco to headline at Gay Pride and then on to Seattle to perform at some club. Marc and I didn't want him around mouthing off as our manager. Things came to a head and we sacked him. He had nothing to do with getting us gigs. Lavern, who'd put us up during the Castro Street Fair, asked to be allowed to come with us to Seattle. Marc and I felt this was only polite, especially since Lavern would be paying his own way; all we had to do was fly with him and see him at the club. (The fact that I didn't really want to do either was immaterial; I would only let myself be so precious.)

Nina suppressed her fury at Marc's and my decision. She had no choice. We all knew—even Sid—that the only reason we'd gotten the gigs was because I'd been in porn movies, not because Nina was cool onstage; we could easily do the gigs without her. But she wasn't going to miss out on a trip to San Francisco.

Neither was Sid. Nor did he have to; his ticket had been booked and paid for by Lavern.

Paying Sid wasn't what bothered us. We resented his effect on Nina. I imagine she knew and disregarded this; it must have seemed insignificant compared to their love. It seemed her loyalties were no longer divided: Sid was her first concern. He'd moved in with her, and it was beginning to be difficult to see her without seeing him. Nina now used the term *we* all the time, something I think she'd wanted to be able to do more than most people I knew. It made me cringe to hear "*We'll* meet you at . . ." when I'd only invited Nina. I would find any excuse to cancel the date. I could no longer picture Nina without Sid. To the extent we could, for Nina's sake, Marc and I accepted Sid, but this didn't mean we had to like him. We were all aware, setting off for the States, of the ill feeling among us, and that at some point it was probably going to get worse.

37

Unable to get four seats together on the plane, we split into couples: Sid and Nina, Marc and me. In San Francisco the same kind of tacky limousine picked us up at the airport and took us to our hotel, which had been chosen for its proximity to City Hall, where the gay pride march ended and where the stage would be set up. A hundred thousand people—more than we'd ever played to—were expected. I was nervous about only one: Luke.

We started the set, but the sound coming from the monitors was too quiet and we couldn't hear our vocals; keeping time with the backing track and with each other would be impossible. I stopped the set and we started over.

Ordinarily when I was so high I forgot most things, but this experience was different. I remember noticing everything in detail, as though my senses were heightened, not dulled, by the drugs. Apart from the bewilderment in people's faces, I felt as though I could see each person in the crowd individually. I studied face after face, looking for Luke. After all, he might have changed his image or hair color. I couldn't help notice that people were playing roles: women acting like mothers, holding children who were being good or bad; punks doing punklike things; men with gym bodies being caricatures of themselves. And then there were the people who were simply audience, playing their roles perfectly. Farther away from the stage, the mass of moving blobs of people blended with the blue sky of childhood. Individually and together these colors and shapes penetrated and lodged in my head.

But I didn't see Luke.

Nina, Marc, and I felt the gig went well, but being on Valium and crystal, I was bound to think that, and if by some slim chance I didn't, I wouldn't have minded. As we came offstage, I signed autographs for a few people who had been allowed back, remembering how when I was younger I used to get excited on Pride Day seeing so many gays in one place and how it made me feel validated. Now, when not performing for them, such large crowds were inconvenient. Getting served, trying to pee, meeting somebody at an arranged point—everything was difficult.

Collecting our stuff from the changing area, the three of us did more crystal and headed back to the hotel to cool off, calm down, and relax. After such excess it was unlikely we'd come down before the next day, so we drank more and did more drugs with a bunch of strangers who had joined us. One of them was a friend of Lavern's, a woman who ran an escort agency. I ended up going to a sex club, meeting a boy named Kelly, and bringing him back to my hotel room.

At nine-thirty the next morning, Marc came knocking on my door to remind me I'd scheduled a ten o'clock interview with a local cable TV channel. Kelly and I were still having sex, and he was my only concern; I found it hard to make myself care about the interview. Kelly had a laid-back attitude, sparkly eyes, a crooked smile, and a Southern drawl. Like Luke. He was twenty-two, slim, and short, but acted and carried himself as though he were big and tough. I found this adorable. We continued having sex.

The phone rang: the hotel receptionist letting me know the film crew had arrived. He asked if it was okay to send them up. Caught off guard and momentarily lacking the imagination to make up an excuse, I said yes.

With perfect timing, Kelly and I came all over each other's faces just as the film crew knocked. I hastily pulled on a pair of pajamas and splashed cold water on my face, partly in an attempt to sober myself but also to wash off Kelly's cum. After throwing the bedcover over a sheet that looked like it had been dragged through trenches and drying my face with a towel, I opened the door.

The crew entered as Kelly left, saying he'd call later. I made no excuses for how I looked or the state of the room. I actually relished how ransacked it looked. I guessed the crew could tell I was high; I hoped that too, would show on film. My nose and lips must have been bright red after eight hours of sex; the room must have reeked. This should have concerned me, but didn't. It was all good for my image. (I'm sure my mother wouldn't have agreed.)

From San Francisco we flew to Seattle and checked in to a plush hotel. My room on the nineteenth floor was filled with balloons that rested on the ceiling and were tied to a bottle of champagne on the bed, gifts from the owner of the club where Whatever was to perform. The window revealed a panoramic view of the city. I showered and changed clothes, and my mood lifted. If only it were as easy to alter my personality for the better with a few glasses of champagne and some complimentary chocolates.

We met the owner, manager, and soundman at the club, and from there moved on to dinner, after which we went to bed early. The next day

I worked out at the local gym, an odd, provincial place. Later, we did a sound check, and later still did the gig. Before going onstage, the owner gave us a big bag of crystal. I stayed at the club until it closed, then went to a sauna and had countless hours of sex with many people. After sleeping through most of the next day, I did the sound check for that night's gig and went back to the hotel to change.

Again we got very high at the gig, and like the night before I went to a sauna (a different one) and have no idea with whom I had sex, only vague memories of events, pockets of images. A boy with a tiny waist, a perfect face, and lips I couldn't stop kissing. A man from Los Angeles with a delicious, fleshy bum, who seemed to think he was the one who'd lucked out. In the past I hadn't really appreciated experiences like these. Having been deprived for so long, I relished them now, and was greedier than I'd ever been before the accident and its endless aftermath.

During this trip two important things happened. In San Francisco, I rewrote the city. The streets, houses, shops, and restaurants no longer reminded me of Luke. I created new memories. In Seattle I did a lot of crystal, an often scary drug, and unexpectedly it gave me confidence. More profoundly, it somehow forced me to acknowledge that I was still capable of feeling confident, and not just superficially while I was on crystal. Ideally, in time, I might even be able to access this confidence naturally.

I knew that this state might not last forever, so I seized the opportunity and called London to tell Seth I didn't want to see him when I returned.

The only times I saw Nina in Seattle were connected with the gig: onstage or on the way to it, and on the plane.

38

Back in London, coming down from all that crystal brought me to the brink of despair. I turned to sleeping tablets, knocking myself out early each night, barely rising to the rank of mess. Finally, I settled into my version of normality.

Marc was now in school several days a week busy preparing a portfolio for his application to the Royal College of Art. Nina was being a girlfriend. David was starting up a company that designed websites. He asked me to help with the odd bit of design, writing, and proofreading, anything he thought I'd be good at. My knowledge of computers was limited to word processing, and I hadn't really done any artwork since college. But I wanted to be part of what David was doing. I learned Photoshop and Illustrator, and found I enjoyed it. Most days, I went to David's and worked until I was tired. It was good being busy and feeling useful.

Wanting to be better than ever, I started taking testosterone again and going to the gym daily. I wasn't interested in accumulating muscle mass; I just wanted to look incredible. I focused on aerobic exercise, using step and rowing machines, and started to achieve my goal. The difference was, this time I realized it and appreciated it.

To earn extra cash—and to see how I felt about it—I rejoined Jerry's escort agency. I did a few jobs and enjoyed a couple of them. I seemed better at dealing with customers than I used to be, and I was flattered that they were willing to pay me for sex. No doubt this would wear thin (it always had before). Ideally, I'd rather have had my ego boosted by someone who loved me, but in its absence this did the trick.

I remembered that American men were willing to pay for my pornstar status, and thought of Lavern's girlfriend in San Francisco who ran an escort agency. When I called him, Lavern was keen on my coming back, saying he'd find somewhere for me to live, and if necessary I could stay with him. (Marc warned me against this.) When I told Gaia about my plans, I sensed that she disapproved, and confronted her. She responded that perhaps it was I who disapproved; that maybe I was projecting my feelings onto her. Be that as it may, I was in the mood for an adventure. A week later I was on a plane heading west.

Lavern had said he'd found me lodgings and everything was set. Upon reaching San Francisco, however, I discovered that the person with whom I was supposed to stay had suddenly had to leave town for the weekend. Lavern offered me a bed at his place, neglecting to mention that he had two lodgers already, who slept in his walk-in closet. It was crowded, busy, if also kind of funny, and I was eager to be somewhere else.

I met with the woman from the escort agency and agreed to work for her. Lavern loaned me a pager. I left the number on phone chat lines—something I'd found profitable in New York—started making money, and felt great. I called a friend who ran a video company, and within five minutes he asked if I was interested in doing a movie. The company was prepared to fit me into their next video, which was scheduled to shoot the following week. Because of this last-minute casting, I'd be sliding in as the third man in a three-way. Conveniently forgetting how stressful I found it having to focus on more than one person in a scene, I agreed to do it.

My confidence boosted, I called Al and went to see him.

It had been years since we'd made my last movie, which—unusual for the porn business—still hadn't been released. Al told me he felt it wasn't "all in the can" yet. He wanted it to be special, and felt that it was in both our best interests if I didn't do a movie for another company that might be released first. He appealed to my sense of responsibility. He had built his film around me and was depending on my image and my reputation to justify his ambitious artistic concept and ensure the commercial success of the project—which to a large extent would be tied to its being my first appearance after a long hiatus. He was prepared to pay me twice what the other company had offered, if I would turn them down. Apparently I had become a much more valuable commodity in the industry. Besides, I quite liked the idea of being paid *not* to work (all I would be required to do was jerk off for the camera).

At Al's office, I got talking to one of his employees called Storm (a name he'd given himself when he moved to San Francisco from Utah), and wound up telling him about my intolerable living conditions. I'd moved from Lavern's only to find that the person he'd set me up with, a doctor specializing in HIV with a largely gay practice, was even creepier than Lavern. I'd never encountered anybody at once so pathetic and so oppressive. He whined about wanting to meet a man with a degree on his wall, making constant sexual innuendoes and rudely putting his hand on my knee as he talked. When he went to bed, he left the doors between our rooms open "by accident." I avoided being in the house when he was there, getting changed and bathing while he was at work. The doctor had noticed this and complained to Lavern, who'd passed the message on to me. Storm kindly invited me to stay with him; he lived around the corner from the doctor, which made relocating convenient. I jumped at the offer.

That night he lay in bed beside me, chain-smoking and showing me his "coolest" videos till early morning, talking incessantly. Luckily, he needed no response from me, because I was in a stupor; everything had fused into a smoky drone. At some point he mentioned that Luke had moved with a boyfriend to Fire Island, which, from my experience of the place, made complete sense. It was the only useful piece of information I remember getting that night. It also answered the niggling question of why I hadn't bumped into him.

Mainly to stay away from Storm's, I spent the next night with Sister Roma, a magazine publisher/graphic artist/San Francisco drag persona/celebrity, smoking crack and watching whatever was on TV. We were joined by a good-looking, sexy man named Brenner, who said he'd dated Luke at the same time I was seeing him. He, too, worked as a prostitute, and he asked if he could hire me.

The perversity of this twisted scenario appealed to me. If I sold my body to Brenner, it would prove I didn't care—about Luke, this man, their joint behavior, or even my own. We headed to Brenner's place, a seedy, slightly scary residential hotel where we partied with GHB and crystal (in my opinion the ultimate combination of drugs for sex). For moments I was intensely, incredibly, believably in love. Physically.

I opened my eyes to behold one of the most beautiful faces I've ever seen. I thought it was somebody my older brother used to hang out with at school, the first man I'd ever jerked off about (I'd had a crush on him for years). "What are you doing here?" I tried to say, but the words came in fits and starts, some not making it out at all. He sat watching me, a serene, slightly concerned, bemused expression on his face.

"You G-holed."

I must have looked confused.

"You did too much G."

I hadn't heard the term before. I'd done plenty of G and never blacked out, but the stuff was much more concentrated in the States. In England, it was watered down; it usually took a couple of bottles to have any effect. You could buy it over the counter in sex shops.

My head began to clear, which only added to my confusion. The more I collected my thoughts, the less sense things made. I was in a fairy tale. The room looked less and less like anywhere I'd ever found myself, even as Aiden Shaw. The man sitting watching me got more and more beautiful.

"Who are you?" I said.

"Jay."

"Where did you come from?"

"I was just down on Market Street."

"What are you doing here?"

"I got a call from Brenner." The name rang a bell. "He said you'd G-holed. He didn't know what to do."

"You're so fucking beautiful."

"That'll be the G."

"Maybe." I looked around. "Where's Brenner?"

"He went to get cigarettes."

I held out my hand to Jay, who lifted his and rested it on mine. I pulled him on top of me, very close.

"You are so incredibly beautiful," I said again.

Though he said nothing, the look on his face said, *Thank you, but you're still high.*

"You seem too beautiful to touch."

"Don't you hate that?" he said, and rolled off me.

"Where are you going?"

"Just taking off my clothes." He smiled.

I couldn't believe my luck. "You've been sent from heaven."

"We'd better hurry then, before I have to go back."

"Don't go back. Stay here with me; become mortal."

I stopped, finally understanding enough to wonder what was going on.

"Hang on a minute. Really! Where did you come from, and what are you doing here?"

"Brenner called me because you had G-holed," he told me again, presumably hoping it would stick this time.

"Are you the G-doctor?"

"I sell it, that's all. Actually, not that much anymore."

He'd taken off his shirt and looked amazing—slim, smooth, perfect. We kissed. He unzipped and slid out of his jeans. It wasn't long before we were fucking.

A key turned in the lock. The door opened.

"I see you've recovered," Brenner greeted us.

We acknowledged him, but didn't stop fucking. Brenner went to take a shower.

Jay and I continued our compulsive, urgent, consuming sex. He must have been on crystal as well.

Brenner came back into the room and started straightening things. Sensing our behavior was somehow inappropriate, or at least out of synch with Brenner's, Jay and I reluctantly disengaged our bodies.

"I was thinking of going over to Al's," said Brenner. "What do you think?"

Jay and I assumed this was an invitation. Brenner called Al, who told us to come right away. Brenner left Jay and me on the street and went to get his car.

"I was worried about you at first," said Jay.

"That I wouldn't recover?"

"That you were a freak."

"I am."

"I know that, but you're the kind of freak I like. You interest me."

"Why, thank you, professor."

Brenner pulled up in his car. "Jump in, guys."

I hesitated. "You promise to show us the puppies, mister?"

"They're at Al's," promised Brenner.

Jay and I kissed in the backseat while Brenner moaned in the front. Strapped for cash, he had put an escort ad in the *Bay Area Reporter* and apparently they'd neglected to run it. The same thing had happened to Luke on more than one occasion. I told Brenner there was no need to pay me for last night. (We hadn't done much, and I'd had a great time with him before I'd passed out, which led to my meeting Jay.) I felt sorry for Brenner, even if he was lying to get out of paying me. I had the feeling I'd probably always feel sorry for him, whatever he said or did.

Brenner rang Al's bell. He opened the door in a pair of shorts, and as always gave a warm greeting. Jay walked in ahead of me, and I looked at his bum.

Smiling knowingly, Al gave me a hug. "Welcome Aiden," he said. "It's nice to see you, finally."

I presumed he meant sexually, here at one of his parties, since we'd literally seen each other at his office two days ago. "Finally!" I echoed.

I was still high. If I hadn't been, I would have been anxious. My relationship with Al was about to change.

Brenner disappeared immediately to do something (some people get very busy on crystal). Jay and I shed our clothes, Al his shorts.

"Jesus, Al! Look at you," I said. I'd known Al many years, but had never seen him naked. I was surprised at how well put together he was. His body was magnificent, with an improbable bum and what looked like an impractical dick, absolutely massive. He looked so much better than any of the models in his movies. "You're amazing."

"Why, thank you, Aiden. You're looking fine, too."

"I love the way you talk, Al."

"You're very sweet. It's nice to have you here."

He bent down to do a line off a mirror. I knelt and put my tongue in his ass. ("Good Aiden," was his response.) When he finished doing his line, he gave me the straw.

"What is it?" I asked.

"Crystal."

"Great! Thanks, dad."

"*Dad!* You cheeky . . . If it were anyone else."

"What would you do?"

"Shut your mouth with this."

Al pushed. I had to open wide to get my lips around his dick, then stretch my mouth as it grew bigger and bigger.

"Jay, you do a line, then fuck Aiden?"

"Okay," said Jay.

Evening turned into night, then into day, then once more into evening. Al directed everything, telling each of us what to do every step of the way. If we were able and felt like it, we did exactly as he instructed, or something approximating it. Brenner kept himself busy on chat lines (the whole time I was with him, I rarely saw him actually have sex). At one point he left the house and returned with two men he'd just met on the phone. One was extremely plain-looking with a goatee, but presumably had some hidden talent because his companion was incredible, tall and fair with the fresh, pure perfection of an Olympic gymnast and the sweetest ass on earth inside his jeans.

Such beauty almost hurt to look at; I couldn't wait to see him naked. After showering, he came downstairs and joined us, and I feasted my eyes for hours.

Al continued to direct, one by one letting each man depart until only he and I were left. We talked and laughed about the past few hours and other topics. When I mentioned Storm and what it was like at his apartment, a horrified Al insisted I move in with him. At the time he had a huge house, so big that if you were in a bedroom you wouldn't know if someone was in the kitchen. He curtained off a little annex to a larger room with a piece of fabric and placed on the floor several layers of the kind of foam used for camping, until it was comfortably thick, then pointed out the phone and TV remote, and left me in privacy—the most I'd had since returning to San Francisco.

Over the years, David and I had stayed with Al often, sometimes for weeks. He'd always liked to party, and even then was infamous in San Francisco for the things he got up to. In those days, David's and my life was very different from Al's. We focused on mental and physical health, reading, eating wholesome foods, and generally living simply. Al was respectful toward us and never tried to involve us in his sexual shenanigans, which was easy enough to manage in his cavernous digs. We never knew anything had happened until, driving David and me to the gym after a weekend of fun, he'd relive his antics in beautifully told, detailed stories that unfailingly had a perfect punch line and—since Al was a gentleman as well as fatherly and considerate—never any names. Yet I couldn't help but envy his sexual avidity and his brilliant way with words. Obviously I'd changed since then. Not only would I be part of his stories now, I'd be involved in their construction. I just hoped they'd still sound like fun, and that in them I'd come across as horny as the participants in the stories Al had told to David and me.

Feeling comfortable, cared for, safe, I curled up in my nest bed and drifted off to distant sounds of pottering, kitchen and bathroom noises, a newspaper being riffled, and other fading indications of ordinary, mundane life.

39

When I woke up, Al was already off shooting the last scene of a video. I found it hard to believe he could work after such a long night, but as the day progressed I understood. Surprised at how energetic I felt, I went to the gym and did an okay workout. This was reassuring—I mustn't have done that many drugs. Then I realized I hadn't come down yet; the drugs were still in my system. I was in bed again, curtain drawn, when I heard Al return. By the time I saw him next, the weekend was a blurred memory, not even worth talking about. Al rose a great deal in my estimation. I'd never met anybody so extreme and open-minded, and yet so warm and hospitable.

The following week was mainly about recovering. Al was keen to finish our movie, and I had to look good for my shoot. Al had booked tanning sessions for me, and asked me to go as often as possible. I went every day; it wasn't my job to argue.

I'd learned this early in my career. No matter how unprofessional the crew, how artificial the dialogue, how ridiculous the sex, I kept my thoughts to myself. How directors wanted their videos to look wasn't my concern. Sometimes the results were so cheesy, I could only assume it was intended. I even found it funny. I also found it funny that the punky, skinny, nervous teenager I'd once been had gone on to become a part of it, *Aiden Shaw*, the British porn star with the big dick. I wouldn't have believed it. I assumed my scene partners didn't find such musings sexy, so when working I remained quiet and focused on the other model, doing my best to make him feel like something real was happening between us. As I became more popular, I was allowed to choose the men I worked with, which made it more likely there would be chemistry, at least on my side. Even then, no matter how much I liked the model, it was rarely enough to compensate for having to perform for hours under the heat of studio lights in front of an unnecessary amount of inefficient crew, twisting my body so the sex would be visible to the camera. It never ceased to amaze me that some directors—especially those at Falcon Studios—thought this a minor consideration. An efficient crew and tasty low-fat food on the set became just as important, if not more of a priority at times than my liking my scene partner. On Al's movie, the crew had been meticulous and therefore incredibly slow, but I didn't mind. I knew from experience how long it could take, and Al had let me do what I wanted sexually, trusting me to be aware of the camera and put on a good show.

Due to the weekend, I'd lost a thin layer of fat off my stomach. (I loved it that crystal had this effect, and couldn't help thinking that it was how many gay men over thirty kept their weight down in California.) After a week of healthy eating and intense daily workouts, I felt restored. I called Kelly, the laid-back boy I'd brought to my hotel room the last time Whatever was in San Francisco, and arranged to meet him for dinner. Afterward we drove to the lookout point on Mount Tamalpais and sat joking and kissing in his truck, looking down at the city and bay. I was tired and ready for sleep when he dropped me at Al's around ten P.M.

I registered movement as I walked in the front door, and popped my head into Al's bedroom to say hello. Al lay on the floor naked with a hard-on. A young man, also naked, stood spread-eagle against a wall, no doubt just as Al had directed him to do.

"Hey," I said.

"Aiden!"

It was clear Al was okay about my interrupting. He introduced me to the boy and told me to shower and join them.

So began another weekend of the most efficient sexual encounters I'd ever experienced. For hours, a stream of men turned up at intervals, acted impeccably, and left when they or we got bored. At around three A.M., Al suggested that he and I go for a drive.

We showered, dressed, and sat for a quiet moment in the car. I smiled at Al. He smiled wickedly back.

"What's going on in there?" I said.

"Nothing. I just remembered somebody I want you to meet." Al checked his watch. "He should be getting off work any minute."

Al concentrated on driving. I leaned my head against the window, acknowledging through a thick layer of crystal-induced numbness how beautifully dysfunctional I felt as I stared at the city whooshing by.

We stopped outside a bar on the Castro Street. Al disappeared inside. It was no surprise when he walked out followed by a slim, muscular, lovely-looking man.

"Ray Goddard, this is Aiden Shaw."

We shook hands, which seemed appropriate after such a formal introduction.

"We were just heading home and wondered if you'd like to join us when you're done here, Mr. Goddard," said Al, smiling.

"Sure," Ray said casually, addressing Al and not really giving me much attention. I didn't mind; I was too high to be concerned, and too busy imagining what we'd get up to.

Ray was soon ringing Al's doorbell. The three of us took more drugs and had sex until Ray left at around two P.M. He had to be at work at four.

I talked with Al for a while, took sleeping tablets, and slept through the leather/fetish fair on Folsom Street that afternoon (which in any case didn't interest me). I woke in the evening feeling perky, probably from residual crystal. Al had another round of men scheduled for us. Some fair-haired guy was sucking my dick when I rolled my head to see what Al was up to. He acted a yawn; I nodded slightly, all Al needed to round off this scene. Alone again, we fucked a little, then Al suggested we take another drive.

He pulled over outside 1015, the club where I'd met Ron after the Castro Street Fair, and lowered the window. "Excuse me," he said, gesturing to the man on the door to come to the car. When he did, Al told him who we were and said, "We should be on the guest list."

Glancing at his clipboard, the man suddenly understood what Al meant by *should be*. "Sure," he agreed.

We parked the car and went into the club filled with shirtless men. I wasn't in the mood for so many people doing disco. I no longer understood clubs. Wiggling on dance floors with my shirt off wasn't something I found life-enhancing in any way. Often it didn't even lead to sex. I wondered why Al had brought me. I tried not to hear the music or see the people, but every now and then I had no choice. A kid, obviously on Ecstasy, stood in front of me, looking like a deer in headlights.

"You're not Aiden Shaw, are you?" he said.

I shook my head. Surely Aiden Shaw had better things to do than hang out in tired clubs too drug-fucked to think of escaping. He couldn't be that pathetic.

Al rescued me. Fortunately, he wasn't enjoying himself either, so we agreed to leave.

Outside, the only flashing light came from a nearby crossing signal. The night air was fresh and cool and quiet. Al's car felt peaceful, huge— a sanctuary. Most significant of all, it wasn't the club. No bravado, no posturing, no attitude. Just lovely, smiling Al looking at me like a caring father in some Disney film.

"More?" he said.

"Yeah!" I said definitely.

We cruised the still busy streets, stopping the car to pick up a man who, I can only guess, was the last man we had sex with that weekend.

40

I slept through Monday and on Tuesday drove with Kelly to Guerneville, a small town north of San Francisco on the Russian River. Lavern had invited himself along, saying that he wanted to show the place to a friend visiting from London. I found it easy to overlook Lavern, so I didn't mind. He and his friend made the trip in a separate car.

We drove with the windows open in the city. Once over the Golden Gate Bridge, we closed the windows and switched on the air conditioning. It took just under three hours on the freeway. We stopped once, because Kelly wanted me to try a root beer float. In Guerneville we went directly to the resort where we were staying, picked up the key to our cabin, and lay by the pool. The sun was hot, the water cool, and Kelly's company was just right for the occasion.

The others turned up looking harassed. There was clearly tension between them; apparently Lavern and his friend had been arguing. I was already relaxed from the heat of the sun, feeling lazy and content, so it didn't affect me. The most I had to do all afternoon was cool off in the pool and move my chair out of the encroaching shadow of the cabins edging across the pool area until the sun went down, when I realized I was hungry and suggested dinner.

Lavern said he'd lead the way, and drove off. Kelly and I followed. After about ten minutes, I was wondering if Lavern was lost. I suggested to Kelly that we flash our headlights to get him to pull over. Embarrassed, Lavern pretended that he was simply enjoying the scenery. Ravenous by now, I suggested we head back toward Guerneville with Kelly and me in front, and stop at any eatery we found on the way.

We spotted a resort with a restaurant. It was expensive, but we decided to stay. We ate on a balcony at the only outside table. The view was fantastic, the food excellent, the wine perfect. Old couples in swimming costumes holding towels headed for the resort spa; after dessert we investigated, and discovered a swimming pool with a covered Jacuzzi. Kelly peeled back the cover; we hesitated, then took off our clothes and all got in. I looked up at the stars and sighed, completely relaxed. We alternated between cold and hot, diving into the pool, then immersing ourselves in the Jacuzzi. Lavern wished out loud that we had drugs. The rest of us agreed we were glad we didn't. Eventually, we dressed, drove back to our Guerneville cabins, and fell into bed like happy, tired children. Before going to sleep, I thought of Ray, the only man I'd met over the past couple of weeks who'd made an impression.

The next morning, Lavern and his friend went searching for a warm spring or mud bath. Like most things Lavern thought cool or fun, this didn't interest me. Kelly and I set off for San Francisco. We arrived hungry after the long drive, and headed for Baghdad Café, walking from Eighteenth Street down toward the corner of Fifteenth and Market Streets. Glancing in the window of a Chinese place, I saw Ray sitting at the counter. I tapped on the window until he turned around, then went inside. Ray acted aloof, but I could tell he was pleased to see me. He gave me his telephone number and I told him I'd call later, perhaps we could arrange something for the next day. (Was I crossing some unknown boundary, I wondered, and should I run it by Al? With Al, more than most, it was impossible to tell.)

I didn't see him that night, and called Ray. The following day, Al wasn't around again, so I met with Ray as planned. I ended up sleeping at his place. The next night we did the same. On Saturday he worked. Sunday was the Castro Street Fair, and he had to work again. I went to the gym, and finally saw Al at his office. He was very busy.

I wandered around, killing time. The editor working on my film offered to show me some of it, and led me into the edit room, where he bumbled and gushed, saying I was his favorite porn star. I wondered if this would affect the final edit.

The credits came up against a soundtrack of chants—unusual for porn. We didn't have time to watch the whole movie, so the editor fast-forwarded, his hands shaking as they pressed buttons and turned dials. I looked at the screen and saw Luke. We were kissing, being tender. I was stunned. Was that how I'd felt toward Luke? I must have repressed it. Was my believing I didn't care about him now a coping mechanism? I hadn't been happy with Luke. He and I had wanted different things. Maybe it would have been different had I been more open-minded or a different person, but this much was true: my fantasy of love had been ruined.

I sat in the edit room confused and sad. What I saw on the video monitor felt personal, private. I didn't like it that other people would see this. Tears filled my eyes.

The editor rambled on about how good the edit was.

"Turn that off," ordered Al.

I hadn't noticed him come in. He glanced at me. Without missing a beat, he told the editor, "I don't want Aiden to see it before it's finished."

A rush of good feelings toward Al flooded me as he led me by the arm out of the room, talking constantly until I was distracted.

We stopped briefly at home to change, then went to a restaurant on Market Street for dinner. As usual Al was excellent company, funny, never at a loss for words when telling one of his many stories. He often chose a word that made me think none other would have been as fitting, always said exactly what he meant and had intended. We talked briefly about the schedule for the following morning. Al wanted footage of me rising out of water gasping for air, me jerking my dick, and general close-ups of my body. I mentioned that since I was jerking off I might as well cum. Al's face lit up at the thought of getting another cum shot.

"The problem with doing a cum shot," I continued, "or even doing hard-ons . . ."

"I'm way ahead of you," said Al. "I've been trying to think who you've liked."

"What about Ray?" I said as though I hadn't been thinking of it before we ever sat down.

"You liked Ray?" asked Al with a mischievous grin.

"Al, you know you're my official matchmaker."

"Apparently," he agreed with ease.

"I saw him the other night," I admitted.

"We can drop by the bar after dinner, and see if he's free."

Apparently I'd been wrong to worry about how Al would react to my hooking up with Ray. Maybe he was one of those rare people who carry no jealousy, no bitterness or resentment when people he knew or had introduced got together. He seemed honestly happy about it.

To make sure I had his full attention, and to show affection, I cupped my hand on the back of Al's neck as I looked him in the eye and said, "Thanks."

"He's pretty special, isn't he?" said Al, finally addressing what I thought was the important part of what I'd said.

"I think he's the best man for the job."

Ray agreed to help. Concerned that he wouldn't be able to get up after working until three-thirty, I suggested that I stay at his place, and that we go from there to the set. Again he agreed, giving me the keys to his apartment so I could turn in early and be fresh for the shoot. I collected a few overnight things at Al's, then packed my luggage and left it where it would be easy to spot if somebody else had to pick it up. (A video shoot invariably takes longer than expected, and I had to catch a six o'clock flight to London.) Everything in order, I went to Ray's, took a sleeping tablet, and in minutes was unconscious.

I woke in the morning with Ray beside me. We had breakfast at a bakery across the road, and afterward, a little more awake, headed to Better Bodies, a gym that had closed down some time ago. They were nearly ready when we got there; my balls quickly clipped, my makeup done, we began to shoot.

Everything went smoothly. I jerked my dick, posed, acted like a porn star, and the crew got their gasping-for-air-coming-out-of-water shot, some close-ups of my body, and, of course, the all-important cum shot. They stopped filming only at the last possible minute. Although stressed from having to rush to catch an international flight, I felt I'd accomplished something important for myself. I hadn't forgot how to be Aiden Shaw.

Storm took me and Ray to the airport, pulling up at the departure terminal. Ray got out of the car with me, gave me a hug, and asked me to call when I got back to London to let him know I'd arrived safely. I didn't like leaving him, but allowed myself to be in too much of a rush to notice.

At home I called Ray, and was surprised that we didn't speak about anything important, yet it felt like we had. The next day, Ray called me, with the same result. Yet another call on day three, which left me feeling horrible, aimless. I put it down to missing San Francisco. We continued to talk daily, and grew to like each other more. I felt at ease. But it tormented me if I couldn't get hold of Ray. Things seemed to have no point. I hated myself like this. It was debilitating. I thought about taking anti-depressants to help me think more clearly. I knew how hard it was having a long-distance relationship. Part of me didn't want to be infatuated again, at least not so soon. The trouble was, a stronger part of me disregarded sense, overlooked reason and experience. My infatuation grew. Instead of medicating myself, I tried for a more holistic solution.

I headed back to San Francisco, telling myself that if anything was good for my mind, surely it was being with somebody I liked who liked me. When I told Gaia I would once again have to miss our sessions, she nodded, leaned her head to one side, and smiled. Was I projecting, or was I right to feel this meant, *You're a good boy, Aiden, not losing faith in men and in love.*

41

I planned to stay three months, the amount of time Immigration usually stamped on my visa, and decided to get my own apartment. Ray said he'd keep an eye out for me, and I thought it couldn't hurt to ask Lavern, who was bound to have lots of contacts as he'd lived so long in San Francisco. He called me back within an hour and offered me the main room in his place, saying his roommates were leaving and he preferred sleeping in the cupboard. The apartment was rent controlled, and he would charge me next to nothing; I wouldn't have to work much to afford it. Moreover, it was conveniently close to a supermarket, the gym, and Ray's. I was dubious about the timing, but the offer was seductive. Ray, who'd met Lavern only once, and Marc, who'd been spooked by Lavern on many occasions, both warned me against staying there. And I wasn't really surprised when I got to San Francisco and learned that Lavern had thrown his roommates out so I could move in. It was becoming clear that Lavern was obsessed with me. But the perversity of the situation fascinated me; it could only be more interesting than not. And I had to admit that I liked being seen with Lavern, in the same way I used to like being seen with a punter—the stranger-looking, the better—and observing how people reacted, first to him, then to me when guessing why we were together. Part of me felt sympathy for Lavern. I could relate to his otherness, his outsiderness.

Maybe I was fooling myself. How could I have any idea what it was like to be Lavern; to see his reflection in the mirror before going to bed at night after having been him all day, knowing that he had to spend the night as himself, too, then wake up and be him all over again, for all those years?

Most days I saw Ray and suffered Lavern. Occasionally I did a punter, but only when Ray was at the bar. He worked five nights a week, so this wasn't difficult to arrange. On his nights off we had dinner together, saw a movie, or went for a drink. Unfortunately, we shared certain personality traits. We both were stubborn, argumentative, hypersensitive, arrogant, and insecure. The only thing in common about our ages, educations, sex lives, tastes in music, clothes, and the people we liked was that we had our own opinions about them. We had difficulty putting up with each other sometimes, but continued to see each other anyway.

Meanwhile, Lavern got high on crystal and underwent comedowns— unless he stayed high, which he sometimes did for days. I only became aware of this because Ray pointed it out. He recognized the telltale signs: twitching, not eating, always wearing sunglasses, sweating, mood swings, and, of course, obsessive-compulsive behavior. I had formed and stopped so many habits over the years, I'd forgotten their manifestations. Besides, I found everybody strange even at the best of times, and tended to let them get on with it. The trouble with Lavern was that his habit started to interfere with my life.

Things had been going well enough. I'd prepaid three months' rent and Lavern was happy to have so much money. On the whole, he made few demands apart from saying he didn't want Ray staying over. When he realized this meant I'd spend less time at his own apartment, he changed his mind. During one of his comedowns, he began reprimanding me for something. (It seemed less about what I'd done and more about him not getting what he wanted from me.) I suggested that he was being unreasonable, which escalated his complaint. It ended with him saying I was evil, that I hated him and thought he was ridiculous. I was angry myself by this point, and confessed that he was right about the ridiculous bit.

He blew up, ranting and raving, looking like a cartoon character. His voice even changed pitch. Rummaging frantically in a drawer, he took something out and hurled it at me. I glanced down, afraid to take my eyes off him for more than a moment. It was a framed picture of me, a naked porn shot from years ago. He'd obviously been hiding it. I felt a pang in my stomach. Realizing how pathetic I found him, he shook his head and shrieked, then left me alone with a resounding series of slamming doors, including the one to the street.

The apartment, still hideously Lavern, was now at least Lavern-free. My first thought was of how Marc had warned me about Lavern. My next was to call Ray. He told me to get out of Lavern's apartment and come over to his place, at least until Lavern had cooled down.

I threw my most important stuff in my gym bag—passport, plane ticket, meds—realizing as I did so that when Lavern noticed, he'd be even more furious. I didn't want to exacerbate the situation, but could I risk leaving anything? I might never return to Lavern's apartment. Increasingly, I found him unstable and difficult to trust. Now his behavior was frightening. I dumped the contents of my gym bag into my larger travel bag.

I closed the door behind me feeling relieved. I'd planned to meet Ray on Market Street between his house and Lavern's. Having packed so much, my bag was heavy and I had trouble carrying it. I felt awkward and self-conscious. Then Ray appeared carrying roses—my knight in shining armor, Prince Charming in crisp white shirt, trousers, and shoes. I appreciated it when he took my bag, and hoped this was a natural response for him. An hour later, Lavern telephoned and said to meet him outside Ray's apartment in ten minutes. Ray insisted on going himself, and was greeted by Lavern flinging the rest of my belongings from the back of a taxi. Luckily, Ray's roommate Joe and I had made friends, and he said I could stay with them for my remaining time in San Francisco.

Lavern became more unhinged. He took to sitting outside the café across the road from Ray's, waiting for me to go in or out of the house. The woman who worked there disliked Lavern, and would tell us when he'd been there and for how long (often it was whole days). Lavern dressed for all weathers. He wore tight jeans cut off to hot pants brevity, high motorcycle boots, a grubby zipped-up bomber jacket with the Trade logo across the back, a woolen hat, and sunglasses, finishing off the look with an umbrella. Whenever he saw us he'd run over, screaming, making little sense, waving the umbrella threateningly and hopping from foot to foot like a scary Rumpelstiltskin. When I was with Ray I wasn't too concerned. He'd been in the army and had done hand-to-hand combat. I was less confident by myself. Ray and I took to looking both ways before leaving the house, and avoided the Castro area, where we knew Lavern lurked. We resented having to take him into account this way, but were willing to put up with it if it meant we got to know each other better. I'd been through too much in my life to die at the hands of a madman. I certainly didn't want this one's face to be the last thing I ever saw.

If we entered or left the house particularly early or late and Lavern missed us, he'd sometimes resort to sneaking around outside while we slept. He left my name and Ray's telephone number on a sex chat line. Ray had to have the number changed. He started going to Ray's place of work. Ray made what he thought were the appropriate responses when Lavern spoke to him, amazed at his persistence and zeal. When Lavern started bugging other staff members, Ray had him banned from the premises.

One day, sometime between four and ten in the morning, Lavern pulled out all the stops, drawing devils, black-magic symbols, and lots of cut-up, disfigured images of me with colored chalks on paper strewn across the pavement. He then pinned them to the wooden wall at the side of the house and taped them on the metal gate, being careful not to damage anything. (Ray could have pressed charges if he'd done this, whereas proving that somebody was stalking me entailed much more work.) Lavern wrote angry, hateful things the length of the block. To finish his homage, he smeared dog shit around the gate and on my pictures. (Did he collect it earlier and bring it with him, or was he inspired when spotting it close at hand?)

When we woke up we discovered what he'd done. We had breakfast at the café feeling surprisingly relaxed, probably because we assumed Lavern wouldn't return to the scene of his crime. After breakfast, we bought two bottles of bleach and rubber gloves and I put all the pictures in the trash, sprayed the area down with a garden hose, and coated it with bleach to make sure the smell didn't linger. The whole business took five minutes, leaving the pavement looking better than before, yet I couldn't help wonder at how much time and hate had gone into its creation.

After that I tended not to leave the house alone at night. If Lavern was trying to affect my life, he was succeeding. The dog-shit incident convinced me to leave the city and give Lavern time to calm down. Surely he couldn't stay angry forever, especially if I wasn't around to remind him. My recent flights had earned me enough air miles for a free trip anywhere in the United States. I decided to go to Miami to visit an ex-boyfriend from about fourteen years ago who had recently moved there and said I was welcome any time. The idea of seeing Jamie made even South Beach seem okay, and the trip something more than just a break from being stalked.

42

Compared to transatlantic flights, I found domestic flying painless and even relished sitting still for a few hours. It gave me an opportunity to mull over things. On this particular trip, my thoughts of course centered on Lavern and how relieved I was to get away from San Francisco. At check-in I asked for a seat in the back row, saying I had bladder problems. (It wasn't my nature to lie, but I'd been pushed to my limits.) For the first time in weeks I didn't have to stay alert, be on guard, look over my shoulder constantly. I drifted off to sleep feeling truly safe.

It was dusk when I arrived at Jamie's apartment. We sat on his deck abutting the bay, drinking wine and talking as the sky darkened and the night air cooled. Jamie's roommate was out of town, so instead of sleeping on the couch I had a room to myself. We went to bed realizing how different we'd become.

Jamie had to work, so mostly I was left to my own devices during my visit. I had a vague plan to comb the thrift shops for vintage T-shirts, get to know the city district better, possibly even explore the Everglades. South Beach was the same as always, only more so. It was White Party week, which attracted overexcited gay men from around the world. Twelfth Street Beach looked like a hen coop, with portable toilets and rows of white beach chairs lined up so closely they almost touched—and men everywhere, looking, showing off, and generally acting out. I don't know how something could be so banal and intense at the same time. I dared myself to brave it. A couple of hours later I admitted there was no point in my being there. I wasn't about to act macho and cool to get attention, or uninterested and unreachable just to get talked to. I let myself leave, and didn't go to the gay beach again. Jamie's deck caught the afternoon sun, which anyway was my favorite. After a morning at the gym or riding his bike, I lazed around on my own, contentedly watching the sun set behind the Miami skyline, and managed to avoid the White Party fiasco.

While I was relaxing, Lavern was hard at work. Checking my e-mail on Jamie's computer, I found that I'd received three messages. One was from a big shot film producer in LA. Unlikely. Another was from Hal Stoker. More unlikely: Luke wouldn't have used his porn name. And there was one from a young fan who'd spotted me in the Castro. This was possible. But the sentence structure in each e-mail was jarring. There was no sense of sequence, the attitude in all was blasé, and the spelling consistently rotten. The similarities made me suspicious. I checked the properties of each message. They'd been sent five minutes apart, all from the same free service provider. Perhaps I was being paranoid, but I assumed they were from Lavern. Hoping to gain respite, I answered them, saying I'd gone back to England.

I assume Lavern had little else to do; he put so much time and effort into obsessing over me. How did he justify his behavior to others? Maybe there were no others. I hadn't met any, apart from the woman who ran the escort agency. She can't have approved of what he was doing. Maybe he didn't tell her, or didn't realize himself. Surely he couldn't have questioned it and still gone ahead and done it.

I phoned Ray every day but couldn't reach him, and he didn't call back or e-mail me. After five days I began to fret. This was too familiar, and tapped into something deep within me. Gaia had suggested that it might relate to growing up in a large family with children close in age and my mum not having enough time to spend on any one child before her attention was distracted by the next. However simplistic, this explanation felt true, as did most things Gaia suggested (whether because they actually were true or merely because they were plausible, I don't know).

Repeatedly and kind of desperately, I continued to phone Ray; if he minded this, he wasn't the man for me. When I did finally get hold of him, he told me that what he minded was that I wasn't with him. He'd been doing crystal. This news disturbed me—I knew how I behaved on crystal. Feeling a bit heartbroken, I asked if he wanted me to return to San Francisco earlier than planned. He did.

Wanting to be able to do this for him—and to make sure he hadn't changed his mind about me—I called the airline. The only flights available were one obscenely early the next day and one five days later. When I explained the situation to Ray he said he'd prefer me to come the next day. There was no point avoiding Lavern if my relationship with Ray suffered. I knew what it was like to want your boyfriend around, even if you weren't coming off crystal.

I lay on Jamie's deck listening to the bay lap against the wall beneath me, basking in the light and heat until the sun began to set behind the Miami skyline, then collected my things and went inside. Jamie was working late and I wouldn't see him. I wrote him a note, explaining what was going on.

I packed for the next morning knowing I hadn't accomplished any of the things I'd contemplated doing on this trip. Wanting to squeeze out every final drop of good stuff in South Beach, I biked down to the ocean. The beach tended to clear quickly at dusk; I could see its appeal when it wasn't overrun with people. I pedaled off the footpath until the sand became too soft, then continued on foot down to the shore and stood absorbing the view, the sounds, the smells for half an hour. As Ocean Drive lit up behind me I realized the beach was cold and damp. I breathed deeply, inhaling my surroundings, feeling lucky to be alive, then biked back to Jamie's in the dark and went straight to bed.

43

Lavern had continued on his mission while I was in Miami. For six blocks down the Castro and eight blocks up Eighteenth Street, he had posted Aiden Shaw press clips, manically taping them round and round anything cylindrical and upright. He must have been collecting them for years, there were so many different articles. How hurt must he feel? I wondered yet again: *What's going on in his head?*

En route to the gym my first full day back, Lavern came shouting, hopping, and jumping at Ray and me. I put on my sunglasses so he wouldn't be able to tell how alarmed I was. Ray and I continued walking, as though Lavern wasn't there.

"I'll ruin you, if it's the last thing I do," he screeched. "I'll make your life a misery."

Lavern had been banned from the gym (no surprise) and couldn't follow us in, but he created a commotion at the entrance. The racket was barely audible by the time we reached the locker room, where I sat stunned for a moment. By the time I'd changed into workout clothes, his ranting had subsided. (The staff had threatened to call the police if he didn't leave.) But he didn't let up. On the way to work, Ray spotted Lavern standing at the door of his bar, peeping in. If he was trying to drive Ray and me apart, he'd miscalculated. He pushed us together, allies against the bogeyman.

I spent Christmas Eve with Ray and his roommate. Joe was an exceptional cook and insisted on preparing an epic dinner for us and his long-term boyfriend. Ray and I bought a tree and decorated it. We ate, drank, and opened presents. My mum called. Everything was the way I thought I wanted it to be. I even didn't take drugs. But like every other Christmas it was mostly disappointing. As was New Year's Eve, which I spent with Ray in his bar, since he had to work. Apart from a break at midnight when we slipped outside to a storage area for a five-minute cuddle, it was completely dull, even though everyone else was in the throes of millennium madness. Maybe the holidays aren't my thing. There's only so much effort I'm willing to put into creating something out of nothing, even for the turn of the century.

Chi Chi LaRue (or Larry, as he preferred being called when not in drag) was up from LA, hosting a show at one of our local strip joints. I went to see him one evening while Ray was at work. It was definitely Chi Chi onstage, although his drag persona was more sophisticated and fashionable now. He joked with the audience, introduced the next act, and came down from the stage.

"Aiden!" he screamed when he saw me in the next room.

We were both excited. It had been years since we'd seen each other. He'd lost a lot of weight and looked more like he had when I'd first met him, but otherwise he was just as I remembered, perhaps sweeter and even funnier. We chatted, catching up. When Luke was mentioned, Chi

Chi's expression changed. He took hold of my chin, his gloves smelling of perfume, and looked me in the eye.

"Admittedly, Luke is one of the most beautiful men I've ever met," he said, then took a sip of his drink. "But he's not worth that." Chi Chi poked his head into the room where the stage was. "Nobody is, Aiden."

My responses were muddled; I wondered what he meant by *that*. None of this came out as words, but possibly my facial expressions spoke.

"I don't understand you boys," Chi Chi said. "You're given so much, and what do you do?" He fell into a reverie. "When I first met you . . ."

I listened, keen to hear what came next.

"You can imagine what I thought when you walked in."

"No," I said.

"Aiden! Look at yourself." Chi Chi waved his hand up and down my body. "Then you pulled out that *thing*."

I laughed. His thoughts suddenly focused on something else.

"Do you still see that guy who introduced us?"

"Danny?"

"Yeah! Danny Cocker."

I winced. "He killed himself," I said softly.

"Jesus!" said Chi Chi, clearly annoyed. "You make me so mad." I knew this wasn't about me specifically, but about some kind of love for his models. "Why?"

"Why him?" I thought for a second. "I don't know. I hadn't seen him in years." Chi Chi looked sad. "Why any of us?" I thought again. "Don't know that, either. But I think it's in the genes."

Chi Chi went quiet. He might have been processing the news about Danny's death. Or he could have been thinking about work. This was something he put a lot of energy into, his mind never too far away from his next project. The music from the stage went quiet. Chi Chi peered into the room again and looked shocked.

"Oh, my God! I'm on!"

He dashed to the stage, was instantly funny, introduced the next boy, and was back with me.

Chi Chi was rare. His humor wasn't bawdy or clichéd (like that of every other drag queen I'd met), just very clever. And very silly. I'd always enjoyed his company, but now I saw something new. As he'd gotten older, it appeared he'd begun to care more. Maybe he was actually the same and it was just that our friendship had matured, or that I was finally able to notice. Or—as Gaia always said—maybe it was a mixture.

I decided to leave when Chi Chi went to introduce another boy. He was in town two more days, shooting a video. We hurriedly arranged to meet up the next evening in the cafeteria on Sixteenth Street where he planned to feed his models and crew, which conveniently was near Ray's apartment.

When Ray and I arrived, everybody was already there, having come straight from the shoot. I recognized some of the lively crew, but not the models, who were quiet, probably exhausted from filming all day. This time it was definitely Larry who turned up. (Contrary to rumor, Chi Chi never directed in drag.) He was completely charming to Ray. Apparently he had the idea of Ray and me doing a movie together. He mimed this to the photographer (with whom I was talking) so I wouldn't hear, but I turned around and saw him gesturing with his hands. Caught in the act, he pointed at Ray and me and mouthed: "You two. A movie. For me."

"I thought you'd never ask," I said.

His face lit up. "Really!"

"Well, we're not sure, but we've thought about it."

"Do! Do! Do! For me!"

"I'd love to work with you, honestly. We just don't know what we're doing yet."

I heard laughter at the cafeteria door, and recognized it instantly.

"Al!" I said, thinking out loud.

He was with one of his photographers. Larry followed my gaze, then repeated in a deadpan voice, "Al."

"Don't," I said, and stood up. "Let me say hello."

"I'm only joking," said Larry.

I walked up behind Al, took hold of his hips, and said in his ear, "Dad!"

"Aiden! What have I told you about using that kind of language in public?"

"Sorry." I wanted to hug Al, be affectionate, but I knew he wasn't comfortable with this. "What are you doing here?"

"Getting takeout."

"Stay a while, please. I'm going back to England soon."

Al looked over to our table and said, deadpan as Larry, "Chi Chi." He turned to the photographer beside him. "We're done, aren't we?" The man agreed, made a date to speak with Al on the phone, and left.

I hadn't been in touch with Al much this trip. He knew only too well how distracting he could be, and gave Ray and me the space we needed. I accompanied him to the counter to get his food. Knowing we were out of earshot, he said, "Is she trying to get you to do a film?"

"He did ask. I told him I don't know what our plans are."

"Bitch! I knew it."

"Al! Be good. You know I'm fond of Larry. You also know I'll do *whatever* you want, *whenever* you want it."

In response to my anything-but-subtle innuendo Al squinted his eyes sexily, switching gear.

"I know."

"That's why you're my favorite, Dad."

His squint morphed into one of his beautiful warm smiles.

"Come and sit down," I said. He followed me to our table. "Al, meet Larry."

"Pleased to meet you," said Al.

Larry sighed.

"You're looking good, bitch," said Al, smiling.

"Thanks," said Larry.

It was clear to me that Al and Larry respected each other and prob-ably even liked each other. Both were incredibly bright men, equally able to make people feel comfortable. Within a short time, they were working their charms on Ray. Al hardly needed to exert himself, as he'd been fucking with Ray for some time, but the stakes were high. Both Al and Larry wanted Ray and me to do a film together, and knew that the more I liked my partner, the better I performed. They could see that I really liked Ray, who incidentally was a very sexy man. Al had asked him before, unsuccessfully, to be in a film, and no doubt guessed he'd feel differently about doing one with me.

I studied the table. Everyone ate, joked, drank wine, talked. The crew looked like characters, but average, too. The models still hadn't relaxed. Ray was glowing from all the attention. Al was busily making everybody feel good. And Larry, out of habit, was making everybody laugh. Everyone was having a great time.

I smiled.

Although I tried to take each day as it came with Ray, I wondered what we'd do when my visa ran out. We were under pressure. When we discussed options, our conversations became heated, ending in hurt feel-ings on both sides, mending which took hours. I should have wondered how this boded for our future as a couple, but once more I was carried away by hope.

Ray disapproved of my seeing clients—whether because he was jealous or because he thought it was bad for me, I don't know. Either way, I thought it showed he cared for me, so I stopped.

Meanwhile, Lavern wrote to the gossip column of the *Bay Area*

Reporter, saying that my movie wasn't selling well. Al informed the paper that the film hadn't been released yet, and threatened to sue if they didn't print a retraction. They did, the following week. I wondered if Al had ever experienced things not going the way he wanted.

I wanted Lavern out of my head. His madness was getting too public. After Al called me about Lavern's most recent escapade, I checked (as usual) to see that Ray's front door was locked, then retired for the night. I thought I heard rustling outside, and checked again, holding my breath and reminding myself where the telephone was, visualizing an escape route through the rear. Christmas lights cast distorted shadows on the first few steps. It was too dark to see much beyond that, and I wasn't about to open the door. Thinking I detected movement, I peered through the glass panels and abruptly retreated—they could easily be smashed— alternately imagining worst-case scenarios and tepidly reassuring myself I was overreacting. It was difficult to know where Lavern would draw the line. Eventually, unconvinced that Lavern wasn't hiding in the bushes, I headed back to bed. My visa might still be valid, but it was time for me to leave San Francisco.

I told Ray in the morning. He understood my decision but didn't like it. I'd also decided that I didn't want to return to San Francisco, even if I was allowed to reenter the country. If we wanted to stay together, Ray would have to move to England.

We changed our minds frequently over the next few days, neither of us able to commit to a decision. Reasoning that we'd both feel more secure if I took the hurdle, I asked Ray to come to London. That was all he'd been waiting for. I understood his insecurity; I'd been feeling it myself.

I called Wayne Shires in London and explained our situation, and without hesitation he offered Ray a job at Crash, his flagship club. Relieved, I called the airline to change my return flight to the first one available. The reservation clerk informed me that it had already been rescheduled—and that I'd missed the flight. Apparently Lavern had somehow gained access to my itinerary. The clerk was exceptionally sensitive upon hearing about my situation, and suggested that I give the airline a secret password, so that nobody but I could make any further changes. I chose *freak*.

Ray needed a week to wind up his affairs in San Francisco, which gave me time to prepare for his arrival. I suggested he not give up his apartment and tell his boss at the bar he'd only be gone four months. He booked his return flight for four months also, so that he would be issued a visa for six months rather than three.

Ray leaned in through the cab window and kissed me. He told me I was the only person he wanted, that no one else would do. I believed him. As the cab set off I saw him mouth *I love you* through the window. I responded in kind. Ray got smaller and smaller as the cab moved down Market Street, until I could no longer see him.

I started to cry. I felt so fortunate. The driver passed me a tissue; I tried to catch her eye, to thank her, but couldn't. Once on the freeway, it was easier for me to focus on where I was going and what I was doing. I couldn't remember ever having such opposing feelings. I didn't want to leave Ray. At the same time, I couldn't wait to get on the plane and start the process of Lavern becoming simply a bad memory.

When I got to London there was a message from Ray. He loved me, he said, but moving to a foreign country and changing his life was too much for him to handle. It was best for both of us if I didn't call him back. His decision was final.

The irony was that without Lavern's "help" Ray and I would have taken things much more slowly. He'd finally succeeded in breaking us up.

44

Devastated, I booked an emergency session with Gaia. After our usual greeting, I sat in silence for an abnormally long time, then poured out my heart about Ray. She did her best to soothe me, suggesting that I put the situation in perspective by remembering how long it had taken, and how much I'd suffered, during and after my time with Luke. At least Ray had had the courage to recognize his limits, to spare us both unnecessary prolonged agony, and to make a clean break. She reminded me that I had David and Marc to help me. (Nina was still missing in action with Sid.) Somehow her clarity got through to me and I felt reassured. What she said made perfect sense. Perhaps I was finally learning from experience.

But it was unlike Gaia to be so explicit. Usually she gently led me to my own realizations by asking questions I had to answer, not to her but to myself. I looked at her gratefully. She seemed somehow distracted. Was I projecting again?

"I need to tell you something difficult, Aiden, and I'm very sorry that it has to be now." She hesitated, then said, "This will have to be our last session."

Suddenly Ray was forgotten. I'd been warned at the outset, and reminded on occasion, that my time with Gaia would be limited, but I'd always managed to not think about it, and certainly the way I lived my life provided ample distraction. Perhaps selfishly, I couldn't bring myself to believe that Gaia would actually leave me.

"Why?"

"I'm not going to be living here any longer."

"Where are you going?"

"Back to America."

"Do you have family there?"

I felt at ease asking Gaia personal questions. Our relationship had gone beyond traditional therapy restraints long ago, and she was so thoroughly professional that I knew this had to be intentional on her part.

"Yes," she said nodding, a sad, beautiful quality to her voice. I sensed something was going on with her, and it was far beyond my small understanding of things. "A daughter," she continued, exhaling air from her nostrils, which meant she was amused.

"Are you tired of London?"

"No."

"Will you set up a practice there?"

Gaia paused before answering. "No. I plan to have a quieter life."

"What will you do?" I pressed.

Gaia smiled, uncharacteristically put her hand to her mouth, then said, "I'll read. I'll walk. I'll do everyday things. I'm not exactly sure yet."

I wasn't about to give up. "You're leaving London to go somewhere to do something, but you're not sure what."

She had the right to tell me to mind my own business, but instead she said, "If you like. It will be better for me there."

"You've got to give me more to work with than that."

It was clear to both of us that I wasn't only asking for an answer to my questions. The reality of her leaving was finally sinking in, and I found myself even more upset than I'd been over losing Ray. Self-involved as I was, though, some part of me was picking up distress from Gaia, which was incomprehensible to me. Not knowing how to respond to my confusion, I settled for the obvious.

"You've been so important to me, one of the most important relationships in my life. You've affected so many of my relationships, so much of my life."

"I know, Aiden."

Even the way she said my name disturbed me now. Suddenly I felt I must force her to change her mind. I wouldn't let her leave without a fight. Putting aside my incipient concern for her, I blurted:

"Don't you care?"

My arrow struck home. She looked at me soberly for a moment, I assumed preparing to strike back. But I did not get the response I was expecting.

In a flat, matter-of-fact tone, she said, "I'm not well, Aiden."

We sat in silence, I because I was speechless. Gaia had always seemed the personification of health to me, in every way the most whole person I knew. It was inconceivable that illness could seriously touch her, let alone make it necessary for her to change her way of life. I realize this says more about me than it does about Gaia, if only how much I had invested in our relationship—which I was now forced to acknowledge consciously (although surely Gaia had had more than an inkling).

She tried to smile again. "I've . . ."

For the first time in all the years I'd known her, Gaia was unable to finish a sentence.

"What's wrong?" I asked quietly, my concern for her finally overriding my concern for myself.

Having come this far, I think she felt she had to tell me, though she probably would rather have held back.

"I have a blood disorder."

My mind spun.

"Jesus!"

I began to cry. My face trembling, my words heaving, I asked stupidly, "Will you be okay?"

"Nobody can say. It's a form of leukemia."

Having had to deal with HIV and AIDS daily since the eighties, I did not consider how brutal it might seem when I said, "Do you have a prognosis?"

But we seemed to have gone beyond issues of insensitivity.

"It could be six years, or it could be six months," she said.

Then she began to cry, even as she continued to look directly at me. This undid me.

"I can't bear to think of you in pain."

Gaia passed me a box of tissues and we cried together, somehow managing to talk about her illness, me probing, flailing, trying to think of anything I could do that might be of help to her. Incongruously, I realized that our hour must be nearly over, and pointed this out—the first time in all our sessions that she didn't look at her watch and remind me.

"I don't want to end like this," she said, collecting herself.

"Me either."

"I think we should see each other again."

"Please."

"Are you free tomorrow?"

I couldn't help but feel a spasm of relief.

"Definitely," I said, still crying. "Thanks."

I let myself out and continued to cry all the way down the street. I didn't notice or care what people might think. Walking through Kensington Park, I hoped that nature would ameliorate my incoherent feelings, but every few minutes a wave of emotion would engulf me and I'd be in tears again.

I returned to Gaia's office having at least slept on the situation, if still a long way from processing it.

"Hello," I said diffidently.

"Hello," said Gaia, her greeting cheerier than mine. It seemed authentic. She was a trained professional, after all, and the reality was that dealing with the situation with me, however monumental it felt on my side, must have been trivial on hers compared to what she was going through.

I sometimes had trouble getting whole sentences out without my voice cracking, but we both maintained our composure and got through the session. As I reached for her door handle to leave, Gaia said my name. I turned. Standing there, Gaia looked more alone than I'd ever seen her, the room so much bigger than when it had been filled with my madness. I said her name in as joking a manner as I could muster.

She smiled. "I only told you because I thought you could handle it."

It felt like she was saying I'd grown up, that the anger that had first brought me to her so many years ago had been dealt with, I would be able to cope with what we both knew would be one of the worst losses in my life. Many people had left me, more had died, but never before had somebody left me because they were going away to die. Gaia wasn't just leaving me, but life also. I was torn between hatred that this was happening and a perverse joy that she respected me and was treating me as an equal, and that perhaps, in the purest sense, she loved me. As I turned to close the door behind me, Gaia and I looked at each other, our eyes wet with tears.

She held a tissue in one hand against her chest. She nodded. "Everything will be all right," she said.

As always, it was exactly what I needed to hear. I wanted to tell her "I love you," repeat it as often as she'd let me before I finally had to go. But I knew nothing could match her perfect good-bye. So I simply said, "Thank you."

I think she knew exactly what I meant.

Part Five
Da Capo

45

I looked down at Luke sucking my dick. God, he was beautiful. I bent for-
ward, kissed the top of his head, breathed him in. He stood up. We kissed.
Was I in love with him? The important thing was we both had hard-ons.
  "I'm ready," I told him. "Whenever you're . . ."
  I didn't need to finish the sentence.
  "Me, too," he said.
  We got in position and the photographer started taking pictures. If our
dicks softened, we made out some more; when we were both hard, we
resumed. Luke was easy to be with, to kiss, lick, look at, and simply hold.
Admittedly, I liked kissing him so much that occasionally I continued even
when rock-hard, and only reluctantly said when I was ready.

Perhaps there are only so many times one can go through the hulla-
baloo of being in love. Certainly this seemed true for me. It's said that

relationships make us grow emotionally, even spiritually, but what I hear less often is how time-consuming, neurotic, and petty they can be. All my life I'd been lied to by every pop song, Hollywood film, billboard ad, and childhood fantasy I'd been fed about romantic love. Yet after each disaster I experienced, some feeble part of me continued to hope.

Single again, my life calmed down. With no lover and no stalker to occupy every waking moment, I had much more time. Life got surprisingly easy. No more drug-fueled group sex, not even a date. I felt too wounded, even post-traumatic. For sex, prostitution seemed like a natural remedy. No emotional involvement, and flattery with financial proof behind it.

I'd forgotten how carefree simple, everyday existence could be, and how well prostitution suited me. Maybe it was just easier this time around. My movie had finally been released, and my porn name was now pretty well-known, which meant I was able to charge ridiculous amounts of money. I found that I was able to treat my customers better and became more turned on, either because I enjoyed sex more or it was sexier to be paid more for doing it.

It wasn't long before I met a customer who began to care about me, wanting to see me every week. Sex wasn't his priority, and I guess you could have called him my sugar daddy. He was well-educated (not to be confused with intelligent), easy to talk to, and even felt okay naked in the dark. Having a steady income freed me to concentrate on other things I liked to do. I learned how to use music programs and recorded new tracks on my computer in the comfort of my living room. I even saw friends, as opposed to just e-mailing and texting them. Relatively speaking, the time passed uneventfully.

Nina reappeared, taking her first tentative steps from Boyfriendland, and Marc and I welcomed her. When she realized we were still there for her, and that life on the outside would be okay, she got rid of Sid. We grew close again. We brought each other up to speed on what we'd been doing. Marc had been accepted at the Royal College of Art, where he was becoming quite a star. This required most of his attention and therefore music took a back seat. Nina had been involved in cabaret-style performances and her voice had developed. It was more powerful, honest, tender. I played her the music I'd been writing on my computer and she liked it. Although deep down I knew I wasn't comfortable onstage and preferred to be behind the scenes, we decided to work together as a duo and see what happened.

We put aside one day a week to rehearse. At our first session it was clear that we both had evolved. We put the word out that Aiden Shaw and Nina Silvert were performing again, and booked a few gigs.

We debuted our act in London, at the Royal College of Art, on Marc's fortieth birthday. Our second appearance was in New York, to launch the Spring 2003 issue of *Nest*, which again featured an article about my apartment. The third gig, also in New York, was at Chi Chi Valenti and Johnny Dynell's late-night lounge/restaurant/bar, Cabaret Magique.

After these three gigs, I knew I no longer wanted to perform onstage. I suggested to Nina that I write her a solo album, which we'd call *Nina Silvert Does Aiden Shaw*. She agreed.

But first I was off to California to do a movie.

I hadn't particularly planned to do yet another porn video, but when a company in LA e-mailed, then telephoned and asked me to meet with them, I said I would. I was already planning to be in LA with a client, and thought it wouldn't hurt to check them out, although I couldn't help thinking people must be bored by now seeing me have sex. So when the head of the video company and I disagreed about something trivial, I told him I didn't want to work with him. Nor did I care that he had presumptuously (no doubt he'd say *optimistically*) sent out an Internet announcement that I was starring in his next "blockbuster."

(Talk about being optimistic—about my participation *and* about his movie!) As a result, I was inundated with e-mails from all the other porn companies asking me to work with them. My favorite was from Falcon Studios: "A premier model such as yourself should be working with a premier company like Falcon." (After my accident, I'd stopped thinking of myself as a porn star—and before that I didn't entertain the idea of being in any way *premier*.) I called Larry to ask his advice, and got his voice mail. "I'm either in the air or on set, so . . ."

I decided to go for it, and called Falcon. Wanting to talk to somebody friendly and encouraging, I asked for Mike, a cool and feisty friend of mine from my early days of porn whose drag name was Shanté. When I told him I was going to be in San Francisco with a client, he invited me to come take a look at Falcon's new offices—his way of making the next step easier for me (unnecessary at this point, but considerate and kind).

I arrived in San Francisco with my abs defined, tanned from a week in the Palm Springs desert sun, and feeling in better shape mentally than I had for years. By the time I called Mike, dropping by the new offices had turned into a meeting. Mike greeted me at the front entrance. Leading me round to the back of the building, he confided that Falcon were keen to do a video with me. I was grateful for this confidence boost. Once inside, he introduced me to everybody (or so it seemed) as we ascended the stairs—and the management echelon—to the big chief's office.

Chuck Holmes, the founder of Falcon Studios, had died, and John Rutherford was now in charge. It only dawned on me as I was led into his office that it was young, shy John, all grown up. As I walked into the room full of people, John greeted me with affectionate, childlike enthusiasm. He reminded me that the first Falcon video he'd ever directed was *Breakaway*, in which I had been one of the models. He laughed as he recalled looking over his shoulder to see if anybody was watching him write down rude things such as "shot twenty-four, first fuck position." Inevitably, we talked about Chuck, and John informed me that, before he died, Chuck had decided that Falcon would donate their profits to HIV, AIDS, and cancer charities. Also, he had funded a new lesbian, gay, bisexual, and transgender community center on Market Street, and the building was named after him. It moved me to hear this. I felt so proud. I'd always liked Chuck, who'd treated me with old-school manners at a time when the porn industry was more underground and seedy, before it had a glamorous veneer.

Though nothing had been said yet about my working for Falcon, now I was keen to do it. It felt right.

Getting down to business, John told me that he wanted me to star in Larry's next movies, a two-part project followed immediately by the second installment in their series featuring viewers' favorite performers, in which I would do a scene. I would have my choice of models to work with. The shoot was scheduled for mid-January. I left the office excited.

Back to LA with my client, then home to London. My father, with whom I'd never been close, had just had a stroke, and I was surprised how much it upset me. I told myself it was because I cared how it would affect my mum. So I was already feeling confused when Ray called from the States to ask me for somebody's number. Before he could hang up the phone, I said, "Are you okay?"

"Yep. Never been better. "

"How come?"

"I live with my boyfriend," he said.

"What's he like?"

"I love him," he said. "He's the best thing that ever happened to me."

I had a nice feeling. I assumed this new relationship was probably as fraught with disagreement as ours had been, but I was pleased to know that Ray was being loved and held and cared for.

Doing another video seemed less about work and making money than it did about habit, possibly even some kind of neurosis by now, although the discipline involved in preparing for it definitely felt like work and was probably the nearest I'd ever get to the routine of a regular job. I had to be so conscientious, eating regularly, sleeping normal hours, working out every day. I even stopped taking drugs, including antidepressants, as they made my dick less sensitive and it took longer to cum. Stopping antidepressants left me vulnerable to emotional highs and lows. This lifestyle seemed unnatural to me—it couldn't be good for a person.

I arrived in San Francisco ready for action and fit to fuck (although I could have begun dieting a little sooner). Mike picked me up at the airport and drove me to the hotel where all the models were staying. My first photo shoot wasn't for a couple of days, my first scene two days after that, so my body could adjust to the time zone. I'd also have three days off between scenes, to recuperate and get really horny.

I'd asked everybody at Falcon, and anybody else who knew, not to mention that I was in San Francisco. The last thing I needed was for Lavern to rear his head. The hotel was in an area he didn't frequent, but I was aware that he could appear at any moment, like the monster in a horror movie. Avoiding his particular haunts, I went to the gym and cafés I preferred, trying not to let the idea of him interfere with my life. Since I was there to work, this wasn't difficult. When doing videos on location, the models are generally kept under high security guard, supervised at all times to prevent them from going out and having so much fun that they're too messed up or exhausted to film. That wasn't the case here; I guess they trusted me to be professional. Except for Al, I didn't contact any of the people I normally would when in San Francisco, and only popped in to visit him at his office.

I didn't feel on form for the first stills shoot, but was comfortable with the photographer and after seeing a few test shots was confident that he'd do a good job. Trent Atkins was being photographed close by and seemed uninterested, so I asked the photographer's assistant to help me with my hard-ons.

First scene. I had some Caverjet with me, bought from a drug dealer who'd obtained it from his doctor. It keeps your dick hard for hours. It was now commonplace on set. I'd never needed the stuff when filming before, but it was available and this seemed as good a situation as any to use it. The potential side effects, ranging from red and swollen testicles to changes in heart rhythm, made it seem that bit more exciting.

I opened the blue plastic box, laid out the equipment, and read the instructions for the fifth time. There were two vials, one with liquid, the other powder. I put a short, thick needle on the syringe. Sucking up the liquid, I squirted it into the powder, which dissolved. Flicking the side of the syringe to make sure all the air bubbles rose to the top, I released them gently and pulled my dick to the left, focusing on where I would inject. I changed the needle for the intravenous one. My hand hovered above the skin. Was this really necessary? Maybe I was scared. That made me more determined. I punctured the skin; the needle was so fine there was little resistance, merely a stinging sensation. I eased the fluid out of the syringe and into my dick, then sat watching. Nothing much happened. I put away the equipment, proud of myself for doing it. Sure enough, my dick began to fill with blood. The veins stood out and the head throbbed. This was a bit premature; the crew were still fussing with the lighting.

My scene partner, Tony DiVincenzo, was pretty—and pretty nervous. I was probably more so, as I had something to live up to. I was also more experienced, and tried to make the whole thing as easy as possible for him. At one point, having already done my cum shot, Tony was kneeling over my head doing his facial cum shot, with his lovely bum hole close to my mouth. Purely for my own enjoyment, I put my tongue deep inside him. (The moment still sticks in my memory.) I didn't feel I'd performed as well as I could have, but the scene went okay. I enjoyed having sex with Tony. It struck me how easily I'd slid back into porn; it had become second nature. I felt like a pro. Larry assured me that it would look great, and it was his opinion of the scene that mattered.

The background for the second stills shoot was a silver metal staircase with blue lighting on the wall behind it. I was still jet-lagged and out of sync. The photographer's assistant helped me again. (What a gentleman.) Despite the fact that I wasn't at my best, the photos looked good.

I finally found my footing during my second scene. I'd chosen Joe Foster, and for the first time ever doing a video I thought, *I can't believe I'm getting paid to fuck this man; I'd happily have paid him.* I felt Larry also knew I'd arrived. He had a habit of talking all the way through filming, encouraging the models. The editors joked that they spent most of their time deleting Larry's comments, but I was glad he did it; it really helped me. Part of the reason for Larry's success—of course there are lots of reasons—is that he makes his models feel good about what they're doing, and that they are doing a good job. Encouraged, they feel more confident, sexier, and generally are better able to perform.

The model I'd chosen for my third scene had to back out at the last minute. Larry asked me if I'd like to work with one of the other models. I suggested Trent Atkins. By then we'd spent time together during breakfasts and dinners and waiting in the lobby for our driver, and we'd discussed the first photo shoot. He'd assured me he had been interested, but was nervous. Larry seemed delighted. The scene had a different director, who let us get on with it and have sex, only telling us which angles he wanted to film from. Trent was great to work with, professional and responsive, and made me feel he enjoyed it, which made fucking him fun. Everything went smoothly, and the director seemed happy.

I was at the gym, resting between sets of working my legs, when through a gap in the machine I saw calves with tattoos I thought I recognized. I got up. Whoever it was, was facing away, about to use the machine opposite me. He was slimmer than I remembered and paler. I tentatively said, "Luke?" He turned around, responded warmly. This surprised me, as did his suggestion that we have dinner.

I'd tried to contact Luke before coming to San Francisco to talk to Falcon. Not having his current telephone number, I'd e-mailed him (his address was easy to remember), saying that I would be in town and would like to meet up for coffee. He e-mailed his number the next day. I called. We spoke briefly and agreed that I would call him when I got to town. I wanted to show him I'd changed, grown up, or at least was more accepting, less judgmental. There were probably other reasons, too deep in my psyche for me to access despite all my years of therapy; the one I was aware of was that I wanted to see how *he'd* changed. Much of that trip to San Francisco went better than planned, but each time I called Luke I got his voice mail. I tried several times, and couldn't get hold of him. I was disappointed, but accepted that he'd decided against seeing me.

I watched him over dinner as he spoke, and remembered how special I'd found him when we first met. It was difficult not to. He *had* changed. He had humility. Things had happened in his life that hurt him deeply. He'd been crushed. My response was to want to help him—to comfort him, protect him, make sure he was okay. I told him what he'd been through had made him more beautiful.

After dinner, I asked if I could walk him home. It was close by. Outside his house I asked if I could hug him, then held him and caught the smell of skin from his neck. Lovely. It was as though only days had passed since he'd last been in my arms. It brought intense memories of feelings, but I kept them to myself. Ultimately, they belonged to me, unless he ever wanted to hear about them. No longer would I force myself on him; I felt too much for him ever to do that again. We agreed to speak on the phone and try to meet up before I left San Francisco.

It turned out Luke was also in one of the films I was shooting. Knowing of our relationship, Falcon had kept us apart all week, which must have been difficult since he had to be photographed in the same spaces I was. At a party prior to shooting, he'd suggested to Larry that he and I do a scene together, reminding him of how well we'd worked together before.

"Are you mad?" was Larry's instant response.

Al, who was much more diplomatic and happened to be talking to Chi Chi, said, "Luke, you can't repeat that kind of chemistry."

"I thought it might be nice," said Luke, "and it would give us a chance to reconnect."

Then we'd met by accident, and Luke was right. Reconnecting was nice. So nice.

I'd had my hair cut after my first two scenes had been completed. Everyone at Falcon thought it looked great, and John Rutherford asked for more stills. That afternoon was the only time I could do it. The photographer, however, was busy with Luke. I told John things were okay between Luke and me, I'd have no problem being around him.

The photographer and Luke were midshoot when I arrived at the studio. I waited for them to break to let them know I was there, then did sit-ups in the adjoining room to occupy myself. When he was done with Luke, the photographer called me in and said, "They want to get some of you two together. You okay with that?"

"Is that okay?" I asked Luke.

"Sure."

Within minutes I was being positioned by the photographer, who wanted us standing side by side with hard-ons. This could have been very weird for me, a possible mind-fuck. Perhaps it was. I definitely found it interesting. Maybe I was just experimenting, to see how I'd feel. It may have been as simple as wanting to have sex with him. Whatever the reason, one thing was now clear to me: I hadn't, as I'd believed, fallen in love with Luke simply because I'd wanted to fall in love and he happened to be in my path. I'd fallen in love with who he was.

"Can we have hard-ons now?" the photographer said.

For about two minutes, we jerked our dicks. Then I said, "It seems kind of stupid, us standing here and not . . ."

I stopped. He knew what I meant, and reached toward me. I stepped into him, and we kissed.

About the Author

Although Aiden Shaw first became familiar to many people as a porn star, he has also directed music videos; designed Web sites; and worked as a photographer, model, singer/songwriter, and interior designer. Praised by *Gay Times* for his "unique insight and intelligence that transforms [his subjects] into engrossing, highly readable fiction," Shaw is the author of three novels that received widespread attention in British and U.S. gay media. The first, *Brutal*, published in 1996, was reprinted several times as well as translated into German and French. ("In a series of short, well-constructed, and simply written chapters the author displays quite a talent for pointed insight into the ways we communicate with friends, family, and self," praised *Lambda Book Report; Gay Scotland* noted: "Aiden Shaw has until now been saluted as Britain's first hardcore porn film star. With *Brutal* he demonstrates his ability to write a powerful story. He has not so much stripped bare as stripped to the soul.") His second novel, *Boundaries*, appeared in 1999; his third, *Wasted*, in 2001. He is also the author of a 1997 volume of poetry, *If language at the same time shapes and distorts our ideas and emotions, how do we communicate love?* which *Mandate* praised as "a gutsy accomplishment" and about which *Time Out* observed, "Aiden Shaw finally proves the pen is mightier than the penis." You can see, read, and learn more about him on his Web site, www.aidenshaw.com.